NEEM

The Ultimate Herb

By John Conrick

NIMBATI IVASTHYAMDADATI

Ancient Sanskrit saying

"NEEM, TO GIVE GOOD HEALTH"

LOTUS

COVER & PAGE DESIGN/LAYOUT: Paul Bond,
Art & Soul Design

First Edition, 2001

Printed in the United States of America

Neem: The Ultimate Herb
ISBN 0-910261-32-6
Library of Congress Control Number: 2001132219

Published by:
Lotus Press, P.O. Box 325, Twin Lakes, Wisconsin 53181
web: www.lotuspress.com
e-mail: lotuspress@lotuspress.com
800-824-6396

Table of Contents

Disclaimer

This book is not intended to treat, diagnose or prescribe. The information contained herein is in no way to be considered as a substitute for a consultation with a duly licensed health care professional.

The information was prepared for educational purposes only and is not meant to prescribe any treatment for any ailment. If you have a serious or recurring illness, please see a competent natural health practitioner or physician. The statements made in this book, unless specifically referenced, could be the author's opinion, based upon extensive research and personal experience.

In the Indian Ayurvedic tradition, no single herb or preparation is abused. Balance is maintained in the body, the mind and in any measures taken to correct imbalance. It is in that environment that the safety and efficacy of neem have been evaluated.

Neem is an herb with a wide-range of properties that can affect different people in many different ways. It should be used only for short periods of time and only as long as necessary.

Since everyone's body is different and reactions to products can vary from extremely positive to extremely negative, use of any product or even food should be curtailed immediately if any side effects or changes in bodily function appear. This holds true for neem and any other herb or new food.

Test your own tolerance or sensitivity to neem in small incremental steps, first on the skin, then in minute quantities orally. Again, if any signs appear of intolerance for neem, stop its use immediately.

More than half of modern drugs – ranging from aspirin to the newest, most beneficial drugs for treating breast cancer – are based on ingredients from plants. Medical practitioners on the Indian subcontinent have produced a wealth of plant-based medical knowledge that is unequaled in the world. While modern medicine has largely ignored the Ayurvedic medical tradition, recent reviews of the proven efficacy of ancient natural treatments are finally gaining respect both internationally and in the U.S.

Among the thousands of plants used in Ayurveda, one plant in particular is generating intense scrutiny as traditional uses for the remarkable neem tree are verified and expanded. Even as this book is being written, new discoveries are being made for preventing and curing human illnesses with neem. Neem is proving to be more than just the "village pharmacy" of ancient India; it is becoming the "ultimate herb" of today and tomorrow.

Acknowledgements

I wish to extend my thanks to the following people who contributed to this book.

Doctor H.S. Puri, world-renowned pharmacognosist specializing in natural preparations used in the Indian traditional systems of medicine, primarily Ayurveda. Dr. Puri obtained his Ph.D. degree in Botany (Pharmacognosy) in 1973 from Punjab University, Chandigarh, India. He subsequently received postdoctoral training at the University of Bath (United Kingdom), and Helsinki (Finland). He was awarded INSA-Royal Society fellowship to work with Dr. W.C. Evans, the famous author of a textbook on Pharmacognosy, at the University of Nottingham, (UK). Dr. Puri is a registered Medical Practitioner of Ayurveda, an Honorary Member of the National Institute of Medical Herbalists (UK) and a consultant to the American Herb Association.

Robert Larson, who spent over ten years developing the first U.S. patented neem extract and provided the impetus for introducing neem to the United States.

Vicki Parsons, editor of *The Neem Newsletter* and organic grower of neem trees.

Dr. David Lee for many of the fine photos of neem trees that grace the pages of this book.

I would also like to thank the following specifically for illustrations and photographs:

AIDS Virus National Human Genome Research Institute: Artist - Darryl Leja

Mosquito lifecycle: Ohio State University Extension: William F. Lyon, Richard L. Berry, Michael F. Collart

Neem oil press: Dr. David Lee

Neem as shade: Peter Strzoc - AFGRO

Crushing neem seeds: Peter Strzoc - AFGRO

Neem flowers: Dr. David Lee

Summary

This book presents the most current information about neem, one of the most ancient and widely used herbs on earth. A major herbal ingredient in Ayurvedic preparations, neem has been revered in India for over 4,000 years, yet is almost unknown to the West.

Neem has historically been used to help the body fight both temporary and chronic conditions. It is this long history of successful use against many diseases and ailments that provided the impetus for the hundreds of scientific studies into the properties and uses of neem that this book details.

This book also provides easy-to-understand instructions for using neem along with credible scientific evidence as to its effectiveness. After finishing this book, you will understand and appreciate the amazing qualities found in neem. You will also be able to more intelligently select quality neem products for your own use.

Introduction

Although neem is one of the most ancient and most widely used herbs on earth, intense scientific investigations of the properties of neem are only now being undertaken. These studies are quickly verifying the efficacy of its traditional uses and are finding even more uses for neem. This illustrates again that traditional wisdom can guide the efforts of modern science in discovering remedies for human ailments.

From almost the very beginning of recorded human history, people have taken advantage of the remarkable neem tree. Even before ancient herbalists discovered the analgesic qualities of the willow tree – from which aspirin is derived – people used branches, fruit and leaves from the neem tree to cure many illnesses. Its medicinal qualities are outlined in the earliest Sanskrit writings and its uses in Hindu medicine date back to very remote times. Even today, rural Indians refer to the neem tree as their "village pharmacy" because it cures diseases and disorders ranging from bad teeth and bedbugs to ulcers and malaria.

Modern scientists are finding even more uses for this remarkable tree. The seeds, bark and leaves contain compounds with proven antiseptic, antiviral, antipyretic, anti-inflammatory, anti-ulcer and antifungal uses. Although major studies to conclusively prove neem's effectiveness are limited by financing and the general lack of knowledge in the West about it, preliminary studies suggest exciting uses for neem:

• *Psoriasis* - Neem seed oil and leaf extracts have been successfully treating the symptoms of psoriasis. It relieves the itching and pain while reducing the scales and redness of the patchy lesions.

• *Diabetes* - Oral doses of neem leaf extracts reduced insulin requirements by between 30% and 50% for nonketotic, insulin fast and insulin-sensitive diabetes.

- *AIDS* - The National Institutes of Health reports encouraging results from in vitro tests for neem as an antiviral agent against the AIDS virus.
- *Cancer* - Polysaccharides and limonoids found in neem bark, leaves and seed oil reduced tumors and cancers without side effects in a number of different studies.
- *Heart disease* - Neem extracts have delayed the coagulation of blood, calmed erratic heartbeats and helped reduce elevated heart rates and high blood pressure.
- *Herpes* - Recent tests in Germany show that neem extracts are toxic to the herpes virus and can aid in a rapid healing of cold sores.
- *Periodontal disease* - German and American researchers have proven that neem extracts prevent tooth decay and periodontal disease.
- *Dermatology* - Neem is highly effective in treating skin disorders like acne, eczema, itching, dandruff and warts.
- *Allergies* - Neem has antihistamine properties that help inhibit allergic reactions when applied externally or consumed as a decoction.
- *Ulcers* - Neem extracts give significant protection from discomfort and speed the healing of gastric and duodenal lesions.
- *Birth control (men)* - In India and the United States, trials show neem extracts reduced fertility in male monkeys without inhibiting libido or sperm production, making it potentially the first male birth control pill.
- *Birth control (women)* - Used as a vaginal lubricant or injected into the fallopian tube, neem oil was up to 100 percent effective in preventing pregnancy.
- *Hepatitis* - Tests show neem adversely effects the virus that causes hepatitis B.
- *Fungi* - Neem is toxic to several fungi that attack humans,

including those that cause athlete's foot and ringworm, and *Candida*, an organism that causes yeast infections and thrush.

- *Malaria* - An active ingredient in neem leaves, called irodin A, is toxic to resistant strains of malaria. In vitro studies show 100 percent mortality of the malaria gamete in 72 hours with a 1:20,000 ratio.

- *External parasites* - Neem quickly kills external parasites and a neem decoction is safer and just as effective as standard treatments for head lice and scabies.

- *Insect repellent* - Studies have shown that one neem compound is a more effective insect repellent than the widely used synthetic chemical known as DEET (N, N, - diethyl-m toluamide), a suspected carcinogen with long periods of use.

- *Insecticide* - Neem extracts have been approved by the U.S. Environmental Protection Agency for use on food crops. It is non-toxic to birds, animals, beneficial insects or man and protects crops from over 200 of the most costly pests.

A key advantage to using neem, as opposed to some medical treatments and other herbs, is its compliance with the first tenant of the Hippocratic Oath taken by all physicians: "First, cause no harm." Over thousands of years, neem has been used by hundreds of millions of people and no hazards have been documented for normal dosages. Only at very high levels may neem be toxic, something each of us understands can be true of anything taken internally.

Many of the more difficult to treat disorders against which neem has proven to be effective include heart disease, diabetes, psoriasis, malaria, ulcers, Candida and gum disease. These diseases do not always respond to the most advanced treatments available through modern medicine. Neem offers its users the ability to take action against these and other seemingly intractable diseases with a safe and time-proven herb.

❧ I ❦

History & Uses of Neem

The History of Neem

Shortly after Julius Caesar established the Roman Empire, Pliny the Elder issued a public complaint: the ever-increasing volume of medicines imported from India was causing a serious drain on the Roman gold treasury. By that time, medical practitioners on the Indian subcontinent had been studying and documenting the effects of hundreds of botanical compounds for more than 2,500 years. As early explorers traveled to India to trade for gold, silks and spices, carefully compiled Indian medicines were also brought back to Persia, Mesopotamia, Egypt, Greece and Rome.

Indian mythology has several stories that relate how neem became a sacred tree blessed with the ability to heal all diseases. The most common story tells of the time Indra, the king of the Celestials, was returning to Heaven with a golden pot filled with Ambrosia he had taken from the Demons. Some of the precious Ambrosia spilled from the pot and landed on a neem tree thereby making neem trees blessed with miraculous healing properties for all eternity.

The first indication that neem was being used as a medical treatment was about 4,500 years ago. This was the high point of the Indian Harappa culture, one of the great civilizations of the ancient world. Excavations at Harappa and Mohenjo-Daro in north-western and western India that date to that period found several therapeutic compounds, including neem leaves, gathered in the ruins.

Among the most ancient surviving documents that have been translated are the *Caraka-Samhita* (approximately 500 BC) and *Susruta Samhita* (approximately 300 AD). These books have been traced to earlier works dating to 2,000 BC and 1,500 BC respectively, and are the foundation of the Indian system of natural healing, Ayurveda. In these ancient texts neem is mentioned in almost 100 entries for treating a wide range of diseases and symptoms, most of which continue to vex humanity.

The *Sarira Sthanam* recommended that newborn infants should be anointed with herbs and oil, laid on a silken sheet and fanned with a branch of a neem tree with ample leaves. As the child grew it was given small doses of neem oil when ill and bathed with neem tea to treats cuts, rashes and the lesions of Chicken pox. Daily brushing with neem twigs helped keep both child and adult free of cavities and diseases of the gums. At the wedding ceremony neem leaves were strewn on the floor of the temple and the air fanned with neem branches. During adulthood neem bark was burned to make the red ash to be used for religious decoration of the body and neem branches were fanned at the front of religious processions. Neem oil lit the night in small lamps. The wood was used to cook the daily meals of beans and grains that had been kept free of insects during storage by mixing them with a light coating of neem oil or by mixing them with neem leaves. Ayurvedic preparations with neem were given for illnesses and neem wood used to make the roof of the house. And at the time of death, neem branches cover the body and neem wood was burned in the funeral pyre.

Neem was so much a part of Indian life that most people were not even conscious of how many ways neem impacted their lives. Long revered for its many healing properties, neem came close to providing a cradle-to-grave health care program and was a part of almost every aspect of life in many parts of the Indian subcontinent up to and including the modern era. But it has really only been since the dramatic interest in neem by the people of Europe and the United States that they have come to realize the value and significance of neem. A movement to protect the relatively few neem trees in India and the many products given by them is growing as the people of India see the possibility that richer Western nations will create a larger demand for and increase the price of neem products.

To address this potential problem, the Indian government is considering legislation that would ban the export of neem seeds – now regarded as a national treasure – and limit foreign sales to neem oil and manufactured products only.

Current Uses of Neem, India

Centuries of proven effectiveness against many diseases have given neem an esteemed place in the culture of India. Neem touches the daily life of almost every Indian, from the poorest peasant who snaps off a twig to use as a toothbrush, to wealthier individuals who purchase manufactured neem-based toothpaste, soap and medicine. Therefore, when manufacturers in India applied for government approval of a new neem capsule to be used to treat diabetes, it was granted in less than 24 hours. After almost 4,500 years of almost continuous use, even the Indian equivalent of the FDA apparently believes that "anything from neem has to be good" (Larson, 1993).

In India neem is rarely found naturally in forests. Instead, it is grown along roadsides and around homes. In the ancient book, *Brihat Samhita,* the neem trees should be planted near the home to ensure good health to those that live there. Villagers with easy access to neem trees have developed many innovative uses for them. It is a common practice for villagers to wash wounds in water boiled with neem leaves. They put fresh leaves under their mattresses and in stored grain to repel insects. They feed their children neem leaves and oil to treat or prevent a variety of ailments including intestinal worms, malaria, encephalitis and meningitis. A paste made from neem leaves is used to treat scabies, external fungi, smallpox and head lice. Adults eat neem leaves to control diabetes, epilepsy, ulcers, headaches and fevers.

Twigs of the neem tree are used daily in India, Pakistan and Bangladesh by about six hundred million people as a natural toothbrush. After chewing on the end of the twig to make bristles, the "brush" is used to clean their teeth with great efficiency. A material in the twig called Datun is under study by several major American University Dental Schools to try to isolate the active compounds that prevent cavities and gum diseases in those who use neem twigs for dental care (Larson, 1993). Neem leaf extracts and neem seed oil have also been shown to be effective at reducing cavities and healing gum diseases such as thrush and periodontia (Elvin-Lewis, 1980), (Lorenz, 1976).

Even in major Indian cities, where modern medicinal products are easily obtained, neem products are popular. Soap made from neem has anti-bacterial properties and leaves the skin cool and refreshed. Neem shampoo controls dandruff and itchy scalp while keeping the hair looking healthy, shiny and easy to manage. Neem toothpaste provides an easy and effective way to use neem's cavity and gum disease fighting properties without having to hunt down a suitable neem twig (Ketkar, 1976).

Skin creams incorporating neem oil are used to control psoriasis, eczema, acne and other skin problems. Face packs and bath salts with neem leaf powder are used to refresh and invigorate the skin after a day in the dry heat of India. A mixture of neem and tulsi powders in cornstarch is used as a baby powder and by adults to prevent prickly heat and other skin rashes (Puri, 1993).

Based on the proven ability of neem to prevent fungal infections, topical medicinal powders incorporating neem leaf extracts or powdered neem leaf are common throughout India. There are baby powders, body talcs, foot powders and deodorant powders that are noted for their ability to protect users from the discomfort and suffering that fungal infections can inflict.

Manufactured Products with Neem

In India, household products used by most of the population are either made in the home from locally obtained raw ingredients or purchased from small cottage industries employing only a few relatives. Products made with neem are primarily made in this fashion.

Price rather than quality is the primary competition strategy for these small companies. For that reason, the raw materials used in their manufacture are usually crude and not inspected for purity or sanitation. A lack of inspection for sanitation holds true for the manufacturing facilities as well. The equipment is often old, in disrepair and may not be adequately cleaned. (Puri, personal communication).

Since there are thousands of manufacturers of these products, brand names also number in the thousands. Although many are the same name the same manufacturer does not necessarily make them. Using a brand name for any standard of quality over time is therefore a problem. Dependence on local and seasonal supplies of raw materials creates another problem. A high-quality product might become a very poor quality product as the raw materials used in its manufacture change with the seasons.

Major Indian Neem Products

In India neem is extensively used in medicines and health and beauty aids. There are a few mid-sized Indian manufacturers of products made with neem that have achieved a fair standard of quality. These products can be found in most major Indian metropolitan areas. Many of the products listed are exported to Indian markets and specialty stores in Europe and Canada, but only a few may be found in the United States.

There are many manufacturers of medicines, health and beauty aids, and pest control products that incorporate neem and neem extracts into products. Only a few of the main types of commercial products containing neem are listed below.

Health and Beauty Aids/Medicines

Bath powders - Neem leaves, herbs and mineral salts

Bar soaps - Neem and other vegetable oils with caustic soda and fillers, colors and perfume.

Shampoos - Neem extracts in a shampoo base.

Toothpastes - Neem extracts in glycerin, chalk, flavors, etc.

Mouthwash - Neem extracts in water, alcohol and flavors.

Creams - Neem oil in various cream and ointment bases.

Face packs - Finely powdered neem leaf and bark.

Powders - Neem powder with talc and tulsi (Indian basil).

Blood purifiers - Decoction of neem and other bitter herbs.

Skin diseases - Neem oil alone or mixed with other ingredients.

Diabetes - Neem powder and decoction combined with other herbs.

Malaria - Neem leaf powder and other herbs in tablet form.

Birth control - Neem oil with Indian soap nut extract and quinine.

Nimbarisht - Ayurvedic pharmacopoeia preparation with neem as the main constituent.

There are currently no large corporations manufacturing or marketing neem-based health and beauty aids. This is primarily because health and beauty aids that contain neem are relatively unknown outside Southeast Asia and India. There are a few manufacturers in India that export neem-based products to Indian markets and specialty stores in Europe, Canada and the United States. Care must be taken in selecting from those products that do make it to Europe and North America. Not all of the products are of the quality and purity standards required in these markets. Many neem-based products were made by small companies that have little or no oversight for sanitation or safety. The products may be made from crude raw materials and may even contain ingredients no longer acceptable or permissible for cosmetic or health products.

For neem-based health and beauty aid products to become widely available and acceptable in Europe and North America, the products must be made to more exacting standards. They must use pure raw ingredients, have sanitary manufacturing facilities and must meet the stringent requirements of government inspections.

Pest Control

Pest control - Neem seed extracts in various forms with the active ingredient of azadirachtin.

Plant fungus - Neem leaf and neem oil extracts.

There are a large number of companies in India and a growing number throughout the rest of the world who manufacture and market neem-based pest control. Government agencies in many countries, including the United States, have approved neem as a safe and effective way to control over 200 different insect pests on both ornamental and food crops.

Neem in Ayurveda

The word Ayurveda comes from the Sanskrit words ayus ("life") and veda ("science"). Literally translated, Ayurveda is the science of life.

The mythology of neem underlies the long history of Ayurveda's use of neem against numerous diseases and conditions. Where the modern system of medicine emphasizes fighting pathogens inside the body, the ancient Indian system of Ayurvedic medicine prescribed particular healing herbs that also helped the body develop a strong resistance to disease-causing agents. Neem is considered a major element in preventing and healing diseases among Ayurvedic practitioners.

The Indian subcontinent has a tremendous number of plant materials from a wide variety of climates. There are tropical rainforests, arid plains, hot deserts, temperate valleys and ice-covered mountains. These areas have been scoured continuously for thousands of years by healers from a civilization that is among the oldest on earth. Their vast array of herbal preparations and medicinal herbs provides remedies for almost every human illness or malady (Dymock *et al,* 1890), (Chopra *et al,* 1956), (Nadkarni *et al,* 1954), (Dey and Mair, 1973), (Datur, 1977), (Jayaweera, 1982), (Rao *et al,* 1986), (Van der Nat *et al,* 1986).

Although the ancient methods for developing new drugs were crude, in some ways they were remarkably similar to the complex scientific techniques used today. Rather than laboratory studies, however, Indian Vedic medical practitioners moved directly to clinical trials. They tested different drugs on different patients to learn and document successful treatments and potential side effects. Of course, these tests took dozens of scientists hundreds of years to complete. However, they had the luxury of unlimited time and the freedom to try things until they found the best solution. There were no pharmaceutical companies rushing to get new products to market and no attorneys eager to file malpractice suits (Larson, 1993).

It is the neem tree that provided Indian herbalists with one of nature's greatest natural factories for different healing products. They use the roots, bark, gum, leaves, flowers, fruit, seed kernels and seed oil of the neem tree for preparations that heal and prevent disease throughout the human body. More than any other Indian herb, neem proved useful in helping the body resist diseases and restore the proper balance to the body's systems (Dey, 1980). The large number of conditions and treatments using neem are the result of eons of work by Indian herbalists and healers. They have been supported by modern scientific studies that continue to provide evidence of the effectiveness of neem in preventing and treating illness and disease (Siddiqui and Mitra, 1945), (Lavie *et al.,* 1971). (Van der Nat *et al.,* 1986).

✿ II ✿

Neem as a Medicinal Herb

Taking care of yourself is the best way to feel good and keep your body strong and free of disease. Most problems with the body can be traced to poor diet, poor hygiene and a lack of sleep and exercise. It is easier to take a pill or apply a medicinal salve to correct an illness than it is to change a lifetime of bad habits. But changing bad habits into good habits is the best way to heal and prevent illness.

That said, true illnesses and long term conditions do need to be addressed and corrected if possible. An ill body drains us physically and mentally. To alleviate illnesses, Ayurvedic herbalists have developed a vast store of knowledge and a long line of medicinal preparations over the thousands of years that they have been healing their patients. With hundreds of medicinal plants found on the Indian subcontinent, Ayurvedic healers have been very successful in treating the diseases of the people of this region. Their store of herbal preparations and medicinal herbs provides remedies for almost any human illness or malady. The neem tree is among the most important of these herbs.

Ayurveda prescribed herbs that destroy disease organisms directly and herbs that help the body itself fight the diseases.

Neem combines the best of both because it is anti-viral, anti-bacterial and a powerful immuno-stimulant. These characteristics are why neem has been so important in the past and why modern researchers are so interested in neem now.

For diseases of the organs, the immune system, the circulatory system and other problems inside the body, neem preparations should be administered orally. For diseases affecting the skin, neem preparations can be used topically and supplemented with oral administration.

First Aid

Neem can be used at times when healthy people have accidents and need a remedy for minor medical problems. With antibacterial, anti-viral, anti-pyretic and anti-inflammatory compounds, neem provides an arsenal of healing properties we can use in these instances (Chopra *et al*, 1952), (Narayan, 1969), (Rao *et al*, 1969), (Bhargava *et al*, 1970), (Pillai *et al*, 1978a), (Rao *et al*, 1986), (Singh and Sastry, 1981).

Cuts/abrasions

Neem's antiseptic and healing properties make it an excellent first aid for minor cuts and abrasions. Neem has also been shown to be an excellent wound healer (Tandan *et al*, 1988). Neem has the ability to increase vascular permeability by increasing the blood flow and by helping the body to rapidly create collagen fibers to close wounds (Thaker *et al*, 1986).

Wash the area with neem soap; apply a soothing cream with at least one- percent neem oil and cover with a bandage. For large wounds, ingesting small quantities of neem leaf to stimulate the immune system is traditional. Healing will be significantly accelerated and scarring reduced by using neem to protect the injured skin and to locally enhance the immune system.

Burns

Burns are not only painful but affect the ability of the skin to protect itself and the rest of the body from infection by airborne diseases. Neem has been used for centuries to treat problems of the skin and to prevent infection (Singh, *et al*, 1979). Burns are treated very effectively with a neem-based cream spread lightly on the affected area. Neem reduces the pain, kills bacteria that can cause infection, stimulates the local immune system and promotes rapid healing with reduced scarring.

Immediately after receiving the burn apply a neem-based cream to the burn with an ice cube. If the burn has resulted in a blister or has turned the skin white cover the burn with a bandage after applying the neem-based cream. Continue to apply the cream until the burn has healed completely. Sunburns may also be treated with neem-based creams. Those that have used neem after sunburn have found that the pain and itching are greatly reduced and the skin is less damaged and peels less than areas without neem.

Sprains/bruises

Sprains and bruises may be treated with an oral dose of neem leaf tea supplemented by either a wrap soaked in warmed neem cream or a paste of crushed neem leaves. Neem as a topical preparation helps increase blood flow to the bruised area (Tandan *et al*, 1990). This helps remove the discoloration and promote healing. Oral doses of neem leaf provide compounds that reduce inflammation, widen blood vessels and reduce pain. In tests with neem extract, aspirin and Indomethacin the neem extracts provided up to 50% more inhibition of inflammation than either of the standard drugs (Okpanyi and Ezeukwa, 1981).

After a sprain occurs wrap the affected area with a cold poultice containing neem leaves or apply neem cream and cover with a wrap of ice. Neem oil and leaf extracts applied topically provide anti-inflammatory and pain relieving prop-

erties that are absorbed into the local area. You should also ingest a neem leaf tea to relieve pain and to internally reduce the inflammation.

Earache

Earaches are usually infections of the middle ear or inflammation of the outer ear canal, which is frequently caused by infection. Neem applied directly to the ear canal acts to relieve the localized pain receptors, reduce inflammation and kill bacteria that can cause earaches. In addition to placing neem in the ear canal, taking neem internally through a tea acts as a general pain reliever and helps stimulate the body's immune response.

To make a healing oil with neem for an earache, heat one clove of garlic in one teaspoon of sesame oil. Let cool to just above body temperature. Add two drops of camphor oil and five drops of neem leaf extract or neem oil, then drip into each ear. Use a bit of cotton in each ear to remove excess and to prevent it from running out.

Fever

Neem has anti-pyretic (fever reducing) compounds (Pillai *et al*, 1980), (Okpanyi and Ezeukwa, 1981), (Khattak *et al*, 1985), (Narayan, 1969, 1978) that have traditionally been used to reduce fevers. While water-soluble extracts are effective, the hexane extracted compounds produced the most significant antipyretic effects (Khattak, 1985). Studies have shown Nembutal to be anti-pyretic while nimbidin reduces the secondary rise in fever (Narayan, 1969).

In a study to determine the effectiveness of nimbidin (a crude extract of neem leaves) as a fever reducer the results were striking. The study required that fevers be induced in rats with a vaccine. Those that developed at least a two-degree increase in body temperature were selected for the study. Basically, one-third of the rats were given water, one-third were given 500 mg of aspirin while one-third were given 100 mg of nimbidin.

Those that received the aspirin began to see the fever go down after two hours by about one degree then slowly rise. Those given nimbidin had their temperature go down by about one degree after one hour, two degrees after two hours then rise by about half a degree after three hours and stabilize (Pillai *et al*, 1980).

To reduce fevers in adults drink two cups of neem leaf tea made with five neem leaves each. Repeat, if needed, after four hours. Since some of the compounds in neem resemble those found in aspirin, neem is not recommended at this time for use by small children for fever reduction.

Infectious Diseases

Neem extracts have been found to be antiseptic, (Rojanapo *et al*, 1985) anti-fungal (Bhowmick and Choudharg, 1982) and anti-viral (Rai and Sethi, 1972), (Sankaram *et al*, 1987). This combination of healing properties makes neem an extremely effective remedy for infections caused by a variety of pathogens. One gram of neem extracts, particularly the nimbidines, was experimentally equal to 800 units of penicillin or .5 grams of streptomycin sulphate (Singh and Sastry, 1981).

Bacterial

Preliminary studies in laboratories have shown that there have been significant effects on several bacteria strains (Rao, 1969), (Chopra *et al*, 1952, 1958), (Sankaram *et al*, 1987), (Rojanapo *et al*, 1985). Mahmoodin, one of neem's many medicinal compounds, shows significant antibacterial activity against various gram-positive and gram-negative organisms (Siddiqui *et al*, 1992). The bacteria *staphylococcus aureus* that can cause peritonitis, cystitis and meningitis is killed or rendered harmless by small doses of leaf extract (Schneider, 1986). The bacteria *streptococcus pyogenes, cornebacterium* and *E. coli* were affected by neem extracts (Thaker and Anjaria, 1986), (Fabry *et al*, 1998). Another bacteria, *salmonella typhosa*, that causes typhoid, food poisoning and blood poisoning, is similarly affected in other studies (Patel and Trivedi, 1962), (Chopra *et al*, 1958). There has been no conclusive explanation for the actions against these bacteria, but research continues to seek the active compounds and mode of action (Rojanapo *et al*, 1985). In tests against bacteria affecting fish, as little as 20 PPM of neem extract was sufficient to drastically reduce the bacterial population (Das *et al*, 1999).

Sore throat

Sore throats may be caused by either viral or bacterial infections. Neem has a major advantage over most other treatments in that it affects both types of infection (Lorenz, 1976), (Murthy and Sirsi, 1958a). Neem compounds have been shown to surround viruses and prevent them from causing infection. (Unander, 1992), (Rai and Sethi, 1972). Combined with the anti-bacterial compounds and pain relieving activity, neem helps heal and soothe sore throats better than almost any other product.

The pain-reducing qualities of neem help eliminate the "sore" part of the sore throat. Most people find that the alcohol extract works very well as a healer and pain reliever. A dropper full of the extract is squirted in the back of the throat and left there for about one minute. This allows the extracts to directly contact the infection. Swallow the extract and let it coat the remainder of the throat. Gargle with neem mouthwash or neem tea made from five neem leaves four to six times per day until the sore throat is gone.

Tuberculosis

Tuberculosis is a bacterial infection that has been thought conquered until recently. New strains resistant to antibiotics are claiming increasing numbers of lives. Those weakened by AIDS are particularly susceptible since, as an airborne disease, it is very contagious. Neem oil and its isolate nimbidol has shown antitubercular activity in sensitized guinea pigs (Murthy and Sirsi, 1958a). Another isolate, nimbidin, was extremely effective at controlling the cause of tuberculosis in humans, *Mycobacterium tuberculosis* (Chopra *et al*, 1958). The leaf extract was the most effective form of neem and showed inhibition at dilutions of 1 part in 80,000.

Traditional treatment involves drinking mild neem tea or breathing steamed neem leaves several times per day. Given the extract of leaves that proved most effective was derived through steam distillation, the traditional treatment has been validated.

Food poisoning

Salmonella bacteria, the major culprit in food poisoning, has been shown to be killed by neem extracts (Patel and Trivedi, 1962). *E. coli* is another bacteria that causes serious problems in contaminated food. It too has been shown to be killed by neem extracts (Thaker and Anjaria, 1986). Although prevention is the best way to avoid food poisoning, once it has been ingested, neem is a viable option for reducing the length and severity of the attack.

Oral doses of neem leaf teas will soothe the upset stomach, help the body rid itself of the bacteria and provide relief from many of the miserable symptoms.

Viral

Neem is one of just a few known anti-viral agents. In a study on neem's effectiveness as an anti-viral agent, neem seemed to interact with the surface of cells to prevent infection by the virus thereby inhibiting multiplication of the virus (Rai and Sethi, 1972), (Badam *et al*, 1999). Similar results have been observed in studies of other viral pathogens indicating a unique property of neem to prevent viral disease (Rao *et al*, 1969), (Singh and Sastry, 1981), (Saxena *et al*, 1985).

Chickenpox

Chickenpox is a viral disease that has an effective vaccine so that it is becoming less of a problem. However, some adults have never had the disease and some children are not being given the vaccine. Both groups are still at risk of catching this disease, though the number of cases is few.

Children who do get the disease can be helped considerably by neem that has been traditionally treated by a paste of neem leaves – usually rubbed directly onto the affected skin (Puri, 1993). Neem alleviates the main problems associated with chickenpox – the intense itching and scarring. Rubbing a neem-based cream on each of the sores decreases the itching, increases healing and prevents scarring. Bathing with neem soap in water with at least twenty neem leaves soothes the skin and promotes healing. Anti-viral agents, like neem leaf extracts, can be used internally for severe cases in children. Mild neem leaf teas or tinctures three times a day for three days will combat the virus, boost the immune system and help reduce fevers.

Adults with chickenpox usually have a much more severe case that can last for a month or more, rather than the ten days for children. Complications are also more likely and scarring is more pronounced. The treatment with neem should continue for the duration of the disease and adults can supplement the treatment by eating ten neem leaves daily.

Herpes zoster (shingles)

Caused by the same virus (*varicella-zoster*) as chickenpox, shingles is mostly a disease of middle to old age. Those infected as children with chickenpox have had the virus lying dormant in sensory nerves after the initial bout of chickenpox has run its course. Decreased immune function as one ages or from things such as extreme stress, HIV infection, chemotherapy, malignancies and chronic corticosteroid use, may allow the virus to reassert itself. Burning pain typically precedes a rash by several days and can persist for several months after the rash resolves.

Neem is a potent immune stimulant that can keep shingles at bay if taken internally during times of stress. It also can inactivate viruses thereby preventing the virus from multiplying sufficiently to cause an outbreak. If the rash does appear, coating the rash with neem-based cream or neem leaf poultice will reduce the pain as well as help to heal the skin. Drink mild neem leaf tea until the symptoms subside.

Herpes simplex 1 (cold sores)

HSV1 is a common virus that almost all adults carry though few exhibit symptoms such as cold sores on the lips and face. The virus is inactive in the nerves around the lips until activated by stress, exposure to cold or sunburn. A tingling sensation usually is noticed just before an eruption of a cold sore. Tests in Germany show that neem extracts are toxic to the herpes virus and can quickly heal cold sores (Schmutterer, 1992).

At the first indication of an eruption, a mild neem leaf tea after breakfast and dinner, combined with topical application of a neem-based cream to the affected area, is recommended. This may stop the cold sore from actually developing. If a sore does develop continue both oral and topical applications until the eruption has peaked. Then continue with only the topical cream applications until the sore has healed.

Colds

Caused by a wide variety of viruses, colds usually confine their infection to the nose and throat, but can spread to other areas causing more serious secondary infections. Colds are better prevented than cured, but increasing interferon and stimulation of the immune system are the most effective treatments for colds.

During cold season, drinking a mild neem leaf tea once or twice a week is recommended as an immune stimulant and anti-viral agent. If you do catch a cold, drinking neem leaf tea three times a day and inhaling steam produced by boiling twenty neem leaves in a quart of water can lessen the symptoms. This will also help prevent secondary bacterial infections of the nasal sinuses.

Influenza

Like the common cold, influenza is caused by viruses. Usually more severe and longer lasting, the flu can lead to pneumonia if proper care is not taken to promote healing.

As with colds, prevention is best, and drinking a neem leaf tea once or twice per week should be followed during the cold and flu season. If the flu does get you, drinking neem tea regularly during the disease will relieve some of the symptoms and speed recovery. Inhaling steam from boiled neem leaves will help the respiratory system and nasal passages fight secondary bacterial infections.

Hepatitis (viral type B)

A dangerous disease, hepatitis B can be transmitted through blood or sexual contact. There is a vaccine available and is recommended for high-risk individuals. The blood supply of the United States is relatively safe and is no longer considered a route of infection. Remaining routes are sexual intercourse, infected needles among drug users and unclean ear piercings. Practicing good hygiene is the best prevention. As a sexually transmitted disease, neem oil can help when included in a lubricating medium. Its immune stimulating and antiviral properties can be an adjunct to the barrier provided by a condom. Once contracted viral hepatitis B is a deadly disease with no effective remedy. However, Indian tests indicate that as much as 80% of the test cases showed significant improvement when treated with simple water extracts of neem (Wagh, 1988).

Drinking neem leaf tea can provide compounds that slow the virus and protect the liver.

Hepatitis (viral type A)

Hepatitis A is caused by eating contaminated food or drinking water contaminated with feces. This is usually something found when traveling to less developed parts of the world. It can also be found occasionally in the US in contaminated shellfish taken from areas where sewage has been discharged either by accident or after summer floods.

As a preventive measure it is recommended to drink neem leaf tea after eating shellfish if there are any doubts about its safety. Treatment, if infected, is to drink three cups of neem tea daily for two weeks.

Mononucleosis

Caused primarily by a member of the herpesvirus family, Epstein-Barr, "mono" attacks the white blood cells. Mono usually goes away after a month and requires plenty of rest to allow the immune system to fight the infection. Neem's immunostimulating and anti-viral compounds can help the body fight the infection and increase white blood cell counts while reducing the headache and fever associated with the disease.

Treatment should begin immediately with a mild neem tea three times a day for two weeks. The length and severity of the disease should be much improved if the regimen is followed.

Fungal

Neem extracts are some of the most powerful antifungal plant extracts found in Indian pharmacopia against certain fungi (Khanna and Chandra, 1972), (Chary *et al*, 1984). In particular, research has shown that the compounds gedunin and nimbidol found in the neem leaf control several fungi that attack humans, including those that cause athlete's foot, ringworm, and even controls *Candida*, an organism that causes yeast infections and thrush (Thind and Dahiya, 1977), (Narayan, 1965), (Murthy and Sirsi, 1958b), (Khan and Wassilew, 1987), (Khan *et al*, 1991), (Kher and Chauraisia, 1972). Compounds found in neem leaf called quercetins (flavonoids) are effective antimycotics (Khan et al, 1988). Two researchers, basing their study on the ancient tradition of using neem to purify the air around the sick, have found that neem smoke exhibited extreme suppression of fungal growth and germination (Upadhyay and Arora, 1975).

Jock itch

Neem seed oil and leaf extracts have been used for centuries to prevent fungal infections in the tropical regions where neem is found.

Using a neem-based powder will dry the area, kill the fungus and reduce the itching. If the skin is reddened, a neem-based lotion can be substituted.

Athlete's foot

Neem extracts have been found to be effective against *tinea pedia*, the fungus that causes athletes foot (Prasad *et al*, 1993). Fungal infections of this type affect nine out of ten people in the United States at some time or another. Untreated, this fungus can attack the toenails and even cause secondary infections throughout the body.

A corn starch powder combined with powdered neem leaves makes an excellent preventive while alcoholic neem leaf extract or a neem-based lotion can be used if an infection has already begun.

Ringworm

Affecting the smooth skin and scalp, these fungal infections are often accompanied by profound itching and redness of the affected skin. This fungus produces circular ring lesions up to six inches in diameter on the skin and can cause loss of hair in patches of the scalp. Neem has historically been an effective treatment for fungal infections of the skin. Early studies verified scientifically that the fungus that causes ringworm is effectively controlled with neem extracts (Narayan, 1965).

In one trial, patients with long term and severe cases of ringworm were selected for study. They had used commercial ointments containing salicylic acid and benzoic acid for over three years, yet had failed to stop the infection. They were each treated with alcoholic neem leaf extract in a carrier lotion. Within just two to three days after using neem extract on the areas the patients were clear of the infection and remained so for the one-year follow-up period (Singh *et al*, 1980).

Washing with neem soap or shampoo and rubbing neem lotion onto the affected areas clears this fungal infection in several days.

Yeast infection

Typically caused by *Candida Albicans* this infection occurs in moist areas of the vagina or on the head of the penis of uncircumcised men.

For vaginal yeast infections, a neem-based cream can be applied with cotton swabs or as a douche with neem leaf extract. For infections of the skin around the penis, rubbing a neem-based cream on the affected areas several times per day, especially after washing or getting the area wet, will relieve the itching, heal the skin and get rid of the infection. Drinking three cups of neem tea for several days will help rid the body of both external and internal infection.

Thrush

Also caused by *Candida Albicans,* this infection occurs in the area of the mouth.

Drinking neem leaf tea will promote healing and reduce the pain and inflammation. Children under 12 should only gargle with the tea and not swallow. For the redness appearing on the skin around the mouth, a neem-based cream should be applied regularly until the infection has cleared.

Diaper rash

Diaper rash is usually caused by irritation from substances such as irritating detergents used to wash cotton diapers and substances found in feces and urine in prolonged contact with the skin. Changing diapers frequently and keeping the area dry will help prevent the rash. If the rash persists try changing detergents or use disposable diapers.

If a rash develops wash the baby's skin with neem shampoo and dry with a clean towel. Then apply a neem-based cream or neem leaf powder. Neem will reduce the inflammation, soothe the baby's skin, kill any thrush organisms and keep the baby's skin protected from moisture.

Sexually Transmitted Diseases

Neem has been a traditional treatment for sexually transmitted diseases. Gonorrhea, syphilis and vaginal infections were treated with decoction of neem leaf and topical applications of neem oil. Men drank neem tea and bathed in water boiled with neem leaves. Women drank neem tea and douched with a decoction of neem leaves. Both men and women smeared neem oil on the afflicted areas.

Studies show that a neem-based cream used as a vaginal lubricant is effective against organisms such as *Trichomonas,*

Candida, and *Giardinella vaginalis* that cause vaginal infections (Khan and Wassilew, 1987), (Garg *et al,* 1993). Other studies have indicated neem can be effective against the types of bacteria that cause syphilis and gonorrhea (Singh *et al,* 1987), (Sankaram *et al,* 1987). These studies are only preliminary but promising and more research is being done in this area.

AIDS

Neem has immuno-stimulating properties for both the lymphocytic and cell-mediated immune systems. When human white blood cells infected with HIV were cultured with neem extracts, the production of viral proteins dropped dramatically. Dr. Upadhyay and Dr. Berre'-Sinousi (one of the scientists who identified the AIDS virus) believe the neem extracts block production of viral proteins, thereby stopping replication of the virus.

Studies of the effects of neem bark and neem leaf extracts show they significantly reduced the P-24 viral proteins and induced in vitro production of IL-1 interferon (Upadhyay *et al,* 1993a). The National Institute of Health, in a preliminary study, reports encouraging results from in vitro tests where neem bark extracts killed the AIDS virus (Larson, 1993). Another possible effect neem may have on combating the AIDS virus is its apparent ability to enhance the cell-mediated immune response to infection. In cases where HIV has not advanced to full-blown AIDS despite many years of living with the infection, some of the patients appear to have the enhanced cell-mediated immune responses (Caldwell, 1994) that neem can help produce. Using extracts made by soaking neem bark in water, Dr. Van Der Nat (Netherlands) determined that the extract produces a strong immune stimulating reaction. The neem bark extract stimulated lymphocyte function that increased production of MIF, a lymphokine that attaches macrophages and monocytes to infectious agents. (Upadhyay *et al,* 1990).

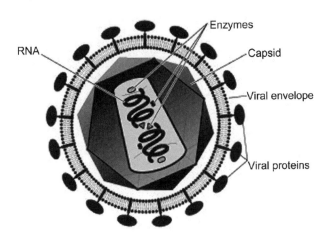

Structure of Human Immunodeficiency Virus (HIV)

Aids Virus

Believed to be the first line of defense against HIV infection, (Beardsley, 1992) neem's ability to locally enhance the cell-mediated immune response may provide protection from vaginal contraction of the disease if neem is used as a vaginal lubricant before intercourse. If even only partially successful in preventing the spread of AIDS, until scientists develop a cure, neem lubricants could save countless lives.

AIDS is a preventable disease. The obvious preventive is celibacy, but that is not a realistic option for most adults. Using latex condoms will greatly reduce the chances of getting AIDS through sexual contact. Using a neem based vaginal lubricant before sex will increase the vaginas' disease fighting capability and reduce irritation and inflammation that can provide openings for the AIDS virus to enter the body. If the worst happens and the disease is contracted, AIDS may be treated by ingesting neem leaf extracts, whole leaf or by drinking neem leaf or bark tea. Many of the complications associated with AIDS can also be treated with neem leaf or bark and creams. Lesions of the skin or burn-

ing sensations have been successfully treated with neem leaves added to bath water and by lotions containing neem oil.

Gonorrhea

It has been estimated that over 1 million new cases of gonorrhea occur in the United States each year. It is caused by a bacterium, *Neisseria gonorrhoeae,* which thrives in moist, warm areas of the body like the reproductive tract, the oral cavity, and the rectum. In women the cervix usually is the initial site of infection, but it can spread to the uterus (womb) and fallopian tubes, resulting in pelvic inflammatory disease (PID). This can cause infertility and ectopic (tubal) pregnancy, which is life threatening if not detected early. The disease is most commonly spread during sexual intercourse – vaginal, oral and anal. If untreated, the gonorrhea organism (Gonococcus) can enter the rest of the body through the bloodstream and go into the throat, eyes, rectum, vagina, bones, joints, tendons and other tissues. At this stage of the disease, it is difficult to detect and is often misdiagnosed as arthritis.

Neem creams used as a vaginal lubricant or birth control may be effective against the gonococcus bacteria (Garg et al, undated) as well as improving the immune system within the vagina. Using a neem-based lubricating cream may be helpful in reducing the chance of contracting the disease, especially when used in conjunction with latex condoms. Lubricating creams containing 10 to 25 percent neem oil were used in the tests, therefore lower percentages may not provide the protection witnessed in clinical trials. Traditional treatment after infection calls for three cups of neem leaf tea daily for two weeks.

Syphilis

Caused by a spiral-shaped bacterium, *Treponema pallidum,* syphilis is not a common disease anymore in the US. In 1996, 11,387 cases of primary and secondary syphilis in the United

States were reported to the U.S. Centers for Disease Control and Prevention. It is easily controlled with antibiotics but many people may get the disease and not know it because the symptoms are frequently mild. If left untreated it may eventually destroy organs or lead to blindness, heart disease, mental illness and death. Like almost all STD's prevention is key, primarily use of latex condoms during sex. As an adjunct a neem-based lubricating cream could provide additional protection, especially in the case of a condom's rupture.

Neem has anti-spirochaetal properties so that it works as both a preventive measure and in the treatment of primary, secondary and tertiary stages of syphilis (Siddiqui and Mitra, 1945), (Bhandari and Mukerji, 1959), (Puri, 1993).

Neem creams used as a vaginal lubricant or birth control may be effective against the syphilis spirochete and may prevent contraction of the disease. As with gonorrhea, creams containing 10 to 25 percent neem oil were used. Drinking neem tea three times per day for two weeks is recommended as an immune stimulant to supplement antibiotic treatment.

Chlamydia

Caused by a microorganism called Chlamydiae, up to 13 percent of women in the United States have Chlamydia, many without symptoms. Chlamydia is implicated in many cases where women are unable to conceive due to scarring of the fallopian tubes.

Neem may be useful in preventing infection through the use of a neem-based cream as a vaginal lubricant. Alternately, immediately after intercourse or if the disease has taken hold, use of a douche made with water boiled with 50 neem leaves will act as a bactericide. A neem-based cream applied internally to the vagina clears up Chlamydia trichomatous infections in one to three weeks (Garg et al, undated). For stubborn cases, supplement with two cups of neem tea daily for a week to attack the agents from inside.

Genital herpes (HSV2)

Before the advent of AIDS, genital herpes was the most dreaded sexually transmitted disease. Herpes is easily transmitted during sexual contact. It produces headaches, fever and painful sores in the genital area that can last almost a month and can recur up to six times per year. It is incurable and has few effective treatments. Neem may be the breakthrough that has been sought since herpes burst upon the scene in the early eighties. Tests in Germany show that neem extracts are toxic to the herpes virus.

Neem has anti-viral compounds that may prevent transmission and infection if a neem-based cream is used as a lubricant for intercourse. If already contracted, neem oil has reduced the severity of genital herpes attacks when applied to the afflicted area. Genital herpes sufferers who have used neem on the sores report a tremendous reduction in the number and severity of eruptions. Drinking two cups of neem leaf tea will enhance the immune system in its response to the virus. Discontinue the tea when the eruption ceases or in two weeks, which ever is first.

Genital/vaginal warts

Neem-based creams have been effective against the human papilloma virus (HPV), a highly contagious sexually transmitted disease that is difficult to treat and can cause cervical cancer (Garg *et al*, undated). There are estimates that 25 percent of sexually active people in the United States are afflicted at any one time and that up to one million people are infected each year. HPV passes from skin to skin contact and not through an exchange of fluids. Condoms and barrier methods of birth control will help prevent an infection by HPV, but breaks and tears can occur.

Using a neem-based cream as a vaginal lubricant during intercourse in conjunction with condoms may provide significant protection from this and other sexually transmitted diseases. For those already infected, applying the cream daily for a month has been shown to reduce the number of warts and stop the itching.

Candidiasis

Over 50 percent of women more than 25 years of age develop vulvovaginal candidiasis at some time, though fewer than 5 percent of these women experience recurrences. Candidiasis is caused by the same fungus as thrush and diaper rash, *Candida albicans*. The body normally keeps the fungus in check but antibiotics and hormonal changes may cause it to proliferate.

Neem oil and leaf extracts are effective treatments for candidiasis (Garg *et al*, undated). Recently, a volatile fraction of neem oil called NIM-76 has been tested for its spermicidal action and its ability to kill diseases that affect the vaginal tract. This fraction proved better than pure neem oil in its ability to kill *Candida albicans* and to protect against systemic candidiasis (SaiRam *et al*, 2000).

A strong neem leaf tea made with fifty neem leaves can be used for douching or use a neem oil-based cream applied internally daily for a week. This will cause contraction of vaginal muscles, reduce inflammation, relieve itching and will eliminate the infection.

Urinary tract infection

There are many possible causes of urinary tract infections, all resulting in painful urination. In most cases the cause is bacteria that has spread from the rectum, via the urethra, to the bladder. Drinking plenty of fluids is usually a simple way to help clear the infection. Cranberry juice is often used for this purpose. Neem leaf extract made as a tea has also worked well for clearing up this type of infection. Several people have told me of urinary tract infections that recurred despite all attempts, including prescribed antibiotics. However, when they have tried neem teas for a few days, the infections cleared up and did not return.

For mild cases neem's antibiotic properties can be delivered to the urinary tract by drinking neem leaf tea made with five neem leaves twice per day for one week. The symptoms usually are cleared up in two or three days. But continuing to drink the neem tea for the remainder of the week allows for any remaining infection to be cleared up even though there are no outward symptoms.

Birth Control

Neem may become the most important constituent in birth control products for both women and men. Neem oil is a safe and effective birth control for women when used intravaginally, injected or taken orally. For men, neem oil and leaf have been tested and shown effective in preventing pregnancy without reducing a man's sex drive. After a single injection of a minute amount of neem oil in the uterine horns, a strong local cell-mediated immune response reaction produced a long term (up to 12 months) and reversible block in fertility (Upadhyay *et al*, 1994), (Garg *et al*, 1994). Clinical trials are currently underway to gain approval with regulatory agencies for neem-based birth control.

Birth control (women)

Neem oil has a proven ability to prevent pregnancy (Juneja *et al*, 1993, 1994), (Sharma and Saksena, 1959a, 1995b). In a test using rhesus monkeys, neem oil applied intravaginally prevented pregnancy without side effects (Bardhan *et al*, 1991). There were no changes in menstrual cycles or ovarian function. An important effect of neem oil used in the vagina is that it seems to increase the antigen presenting ability of the uterine tract. This activation of the local immune cell population has a direct spermicidal effect without apparent side effect.

Neem oil and neem extracts have the added benefit of preventing vaginal and sexually transmitted diseases (Upadhyay *et al*, 1990), (Garg *et al*, undated), (Lal *et al*, 1985), (Sinha *et al*, 1984a).

Years of study in India by some of the world's leading contraceptive scientists resulted in the development of a neem-based polyherbal vaginal cream that has both spermicidal and anti-microbial action. The cream combines 10 to 25 per cent neem oil, a surfactant (like sodium lauryl sulphate used in many shampoos) and quinine hydrochloride, a synthetic flavoring agent used in bitters and fruit flavorings for beverages. Initial tests of its effectiveness showed that it compared favorably with the chemical-based foams and gels. It was safer and easier to use, caused no irritation or discomfort, was nearly 100% effective, and was therefore used more frequently than the foam or gel spermicides (Garg *et al*, 1993). The effect does not appear to be hormonal and is considered a safe and effective alternative to other methods that use hormones (Prakash *et al*, 1988), (Mateenuddin *et al*, 1986).

During the Phase I clinical trials using the cream in India it was discovered that the cream had tremendous benefits for decreasing sexually transmitted diseases in addition to its birth control properties. Neem oil and leaf extracts have spermicidal, anti-microbial, anti-fungal and anti-viral properties. But most importantly they enhance the local immune response, particularly the TH1 type response (See the section on HIV for more details). Therefore, neem and neem extracts can prevent pregnancy and prevent diseases caused by *Candida albicans*, *C. tropicalis*, *Neisseria gonorrhoeae*, the multidrug-resistant *Staphylococcus aureus* and urinary tract *Escherichia coli*, Herpes simplex-2 and HIV-1 (Talwar *et al*, 1997b).

In India, vaginal creams and suppositories made with neem oil are quickly becoming the birth control method of choice (Paranjapo and Paranjapo, 1993), (Garg *et al*, 1993), (Riar *et al*, 1993). They are non-irritating and easy to use while almost 100 percent effective. The studies leading to the development of these products proved that neem oil killed sperm in the vagina within thirty seconds and was effective for up to five hours. Most spermicidal creams must be reapplied at least every hour (Sinha *et al*, 1984a).

Certain purified extracts of neem have also been tested to determine if distinct compounds can be more effective than simple neem oil for birth control. When tested against human sperm, the neem extract (sodium nimbidinate) at 1000 mg was able to kill all sperm in just 5 minutes and required only 30 minutes at a 250-mg level. (Sharma *et al*, 1959a), (Khare, 1984), (Lal *et al*, 1987), (Riar *et al*, 1988), (Sinha *et al*, 1984b). But simple neem oil has been shown to work well both before and after sex while some purified extracts only worked before sex as a preventive (Riar et al, 1991). After the testing of many neem compounds it appears as though neem oil is the most effective form of neem for birth control, particularly hexane extracted neem oil.

Neem oil has been found to prevent implantation and may even have an abortifacient effect similar to pennyroyal, juniper berries, wild ginger, myrrh and angelica. The effects were seen as many as ten days after fertilization in rats though it was most effective at no more than three days (Sinha *et al*, 1984b), (Lal *et al*, 1985). In a study on rats, neem oil was given orally eight to ten days after implantation of the fetus on the uterine wall. In all cases, by day 15, the embryos were all completely reabsorbed by the body. The animals regained fertility on the next cycle, showing no physical problems. Detailed study of the rats revealed increased levels of gamma interferon in the uterus indicating that neem oil enhanced the local immune response in the uterus. (Mukherjee *et al*, 1996). Post coital use of neem oil as birth control does not appear to work by hormonal changes but produces changes in the organs that make pregnancy no longer viable (Tewari, 1989), (Bardhan *et al*, 1991). By being a non-hormonal post-coital contraceptive it is expected that neem oil would have fewer side effects (Prakash *et al*, 1988).

A distillate of hexane extracted neem oil, a mixture of six primary active fractions, resulted in a product that could completely abrogate pregnancy in rodents with no apparent side effects. The neem compound mixture caused the activation of

T-lymphocyte cells of CD8+ subtype and phagocytic cells followed by an elevation in cytokines gamma-interferon and tumor necrosis factor alpha(TNF). The experiment indicates that an active fraction of hexane extracted neem oil can be taken orally for early post implantation contraception based on cell mediated immune reactions (Mukherjee *et al*, 1999).

I doubt that, given all of the options for birth control available to most people in the more affluent parts of the world, a homemade neem-based cream preparation would be a first choice. However, neem has the additional properties of strengthening the immune system in the vaginal tract and acting as an antibacterial and antiviral agent without irritating the vaginal tract as so many of the commercial spermicidal creams and lubricants can. As for ingesting neem for contraception – until a high quality neem oil with proven purity is developed neem oil is not recommended for any internal consumption in any appreciable amounts.

To prevent pregnancy use a water based vaginal lubricant with ten-percent neem oil added. Apply before intercourse to give the surface of the vaginal wall time to become coated with the material. If there was no neem lubricant available during intercourse applying the lubricant soon after intercourse will prevent implantation, however, careful consideration must be given to the implications of this procedure.

Birth control (men)

Neem may become the first truly effective birth control "pill" for men (Riar, 1988). Neem leaf tablets ingested for one month produced reversible male antifertility without affecting sperm production or libido (Deshpande, 1980), (Sadre, 1984). In India and the United States, exploratory trials show neem extracts reduced fertility in male monkeys without inhibiting libido or sperm production (Sharma *et al*, 1987) and ethanol extracts of neem leaf given to male rats caused females who mated with them to be unable to become pregnant as long as the males took the extract (Choudhary, 1990).

In a test of neem's birth control effects with members of the Indian Army, daily oral doses of several drops of neem seed oil in gelatin capsules were given to twenty married soldiers. The effect took six weeks to become 100 percent effective, it remained effective during the entire year of the trial and was reversed six weeks after the subjects stopped taking the capsules. During this time the men experienced no adverse side effects and retained their normal capabilities and desires (National Research Council, 1992). There were no pregnancies of any of the wives during the study.

For long term birth control for men it appears that a very minute amount of neem oil injected in the vas deferens provides up to eight months of birth control. The tests revealed no obstructions, no change in testosterone production and no anti-sperm antibodies. The local lymph nodes showed increased ability to respond to infections, indicating an immune response may be responsible for the birth control effect in men as it is in women (Upadhyay, 1993b).

Taking 30 drops of neem leaf extracted with alcohol or two grams of neem leaf daily for six weeks will reduce the motility of sperm thereby preventing them from reaching and impregnating the egg. The neem material must be taken daily for the effect to continue. Approximately six weeks after ceasing consumption, sperm motility should return and the birth control effect will be reversed.

Skin Diseases

According to Ayurveda, skin diseases are caused by the excess of sugary substances in the body. To counteract them, the opposite of sugar – bitter – is prescribed (Puri, 1993). Neem is an herb of choice for skin diseases because of its bitter principles and has proven to be highly effective in treating disorders like psoriasis, acne, eczema, itching, dandruff and warts (Ghosh, 1987). Neem has been used for treating all sorts of skin problems for thousands of years and is considered to be equal, or even superior, to aloe in its healing properties.

Psoriasis

Psoriasis is a noncontagious skin disorder that usually appears as inflamed swollen skin lesions covered with a silvery white scale. It has no cure and not all treatments work for each individual, often requiring people to combine therapies in order to discover the regimen that is most effective. Psoriasis on its own can come and go often with long periods of remission. In most cases, however, psoriasis is persistent.

Neem oil is probably the best product currently available for treating psoriasis. It moisturizes and protects the skin while it helps heal the lesions, scaling and irritation. Experiments and reports from patients with psoriasis have shown taking neem leaf orally, combined with topical treatment with neem extracts and neem seed oil, appear to be at least as effective as coal tar and cortisone in treating psoriasis. (Narayan, 1978).

In a case study a patient with severe psoriasis was given neem extract (nimbidin) three times a day and the skin treated with nimbidin mixed in coconut oil. The treatments lasted less than three months, stopped the itching and redness and continued to improve the condition of the skin for the duration of treatment. The final result of the treatments was the complete disappearance of the signs of psoriasis. They produced no noticeable side effects (Rajasekbaran *et al*, 1980). Anecdotal reports indicate that improvements are faster when the areas treated with neem are also exposed to sunlight.

The usual treatment for psoriasis involves either coal tar or cortisone. Coal tar products are messy and smell, and cortisone can thin the skin after repeated use. Neem has neither drawback. Topical applications of neem are easy and inexpensive, and since it is usually oil or cream based, neem helps to lubricate the skin. There are no unpleasant smells or stains on clothing, and its antibacterial and anti-viral compounds help prevent infections. It also can be used for extended periods of time without side effects. Neem can also take the place of oral medications and injections that may have strong side effects or cause liver damage or birth defects. It is perhaps the best and safest alternative for treating psoriasis.

Some medications use salicylate to treat psoriasis and other skin disorders. In a study of the potential side effects of this treatment it was found that those with sores on the skin were able to absorb salicylate into their system very easily. In one severe case a 70-year-old man with psoriasis being treated with a topical salicylic acid developed encephalopathy, respiratory alkalosis and metabolic acidosis. Dialysis was able to lower the salicylic acid and restore normal metabolism (Pertoldi *et al*, 1999). With side effects such as this neem can provide a safe alternative for treating psoriasis and other skin disorders.

Washing the skin with a neem soap (shampoo if the area is sensitive) to remove dead cells and to kill bacteria is a good first step in the process of treating psoriasis. To soothe the skin you can add twenty neem leaves to the tub before turning on the hot water and soak in the neem filled water. After patting dry, apply a neem-based cream or lotion to the troubled areas. To enhance the effectiveness, oral doses of neem leaf work internally to produces quicker results than topical creams alone.

Vitiligo

Vitiligo is believed to be an autoimmune disorder that causes patches of skin to lose their color. While it is most obvious in dark skinned people it occurs in about .5 percent of the population regardless of race. The only treatments are exposures to sunlight (or PUVA) or corticosteroid drugs. But these treatments are often not effective.

Oral doses of neem were tested on fifteen patients with at least one-year history of vitiligo. In addition to the oral neem doses a cream of several herbs was applied to the patches then exposed to sunlight. The results showed that after ninety days 25% of the patients showed complete relief and another 60% showed mild to moderate relief. There were no adverse reactions to any of the participants in this group. Those that were able to continue the treatment the longest obtained the most improvement indicating that complete improvement could have been obtained by the participants had they all stayed on the regimen (Nair *et al*, 1987).

The dosage in the test was four grams of neem leaves three times a day, preferably before each meal. External application of the cream in the study is impracticable in the west, as the ingredients are almost impossible to obtain. However, in other studies the use of neem (leaves and bark) internally without the need for any applications to the skin worked well (Basu, 1956).

Given the immune stimulating properties of neem oil and its effects on other skin problems it is quite possible that neem oil applied to the affected area in conjunction with oral doses of neem leaf or bark could aid in the reversal of the discoloration caused by vitiligo.

Eczema

The broad range of beneficial effects neem has on skin makes it one of the better treatments for eczema (dermatitis). Though neem oil is preferred because of the concentration of active compounds, topical applications of even the weaker leaf extracts have cured acute eczema (Singh *et al*, 1979).

To relieve the intense itching and reddening of eczema, wash the affected skin with a neem soap or a shampoo to gently cleanse and kill any infectious bacteria. For a general therapeutic soak, add commercial bath salts and neem leaf or extracts to the bath water. For specific areas of the body, wash with neem soap or shampoo, then apply a neem-based cream to the area. For difficult cases, drink a mild neem leaf tea with a quarter teaspoon of pepper twice a day until the symptoms disappear.

Wrinkles

Creams or lotions containing neem oil can be used to prevent wrinkles by providing a natural skin protectant and moisturizer to the skin. Antibacterial compounds in neem protect the skin while immune stimulating compounds help deeper layers of the skin fight any pathogens below the surface. These neem compounds help healthy skin retain its suppleness (Puri, 1993).

After washing and drying the skin, rub a few drops of neem based cream on areas that are particularly susceptible to drying and wrinkles. To supplement the beneficial effects of neem oil, apply a face pack made from neem bark and leaves. As the face pack dries, the soothing compounds of neem are absorbed into the skin. This helps to reduce wrinkles and will make the skin feel smoother and appear younger. It is an astringent mixture that tightens the skin and is particularly useful for hypersensitive people.

Acne

Acne is usually an inflamed hair follicle caused by a blockage of sebum (oil produced by the skin). Neem kills the bacteria that cause the acne and reduces the inflammation that makes it so noticeable. Neem-based creams have even improved the appearance of people who have reddened skin from acne that ended years before.

To prevent and heal acne, first wash with neem soap, then use a neem face pack to soothe and tighten the skin. Finally, apply a neem-based lotion or cream to moisturize and condition the skin. Neem leaf (one gram) taken internally daily counteracts excess sugar in the body and helps reduce acne.

Dry skin

Dry skin is the result of age and how well we have protected our skin from the environment. With age the dermis is less able to retain water and fat; oil glands are unable to produce sufficient oil and fewer supporting fibers, collagen and elastin, are produced. Tiny capillaries that feed the skin close off, depriving the skin of oxygen and nutrients. This combination of conditions produces dry skin. Neem oil applied to the skin replenishes the oil that is missing, helps retain water in the skin and helps stimulate the production of collagen. The tiny capillaries are dilated by neem compounds renewing blood supply to the skin. The skin therefore begins to reverse the conditions that cause dry skin and the added oil and retained water make the skin feel softer and smoother.

> *For mildly dry skin wash with neem soap, then apply a neem lotion as a moisturizer. For severe dry skin, after washing, apply neem cream and repeat several times daily until the skin has recovered its natural balance.*

Dandruff

Usually associated with imbalance in hormones, infections, or diets rich in fats and sweets, dandruff can only be controlled, not cured. As with other forms of dermatitis, neem is the herb of choice for controlling dandruff. Internally, neem compounds counteract excessive sweets and seem to provide balance to hormones (Puri, 1993).

> *To treat dandruff, apply a neem-based cream to the scalp shortly before bathing. This will loosen the scaly flakes and soften the scalp. Using a neem shampoo, usually with extract of neem leaf, will remove the loosened flakes and kill any pathogen that may attack the scalp. After the bath, apply a very small amount of neem cream to the scalp and towel dry the hair to remove any excess. Taking neem leaf tea after an especially fatty or sugary meal will also help balance the body, which can help prevent dandruff.*

Itchy scalp

Itchy scalps can be caused by any number of things, ranging from allergies and dandruff to mites.

> *Washing the scalp with a neem shampoo and applying a*

small amount of neem lotion to the scalp afterwards will relieve each of these problems.

Skin ulcers

Skin ulcers most commonly occur on the leg due to inadequate blood supply or drainage. The destruction of the surface tissue can be shallow or deep and is usually inflamed and painful.

Like any other open wound they should be washed with a neem soap and covered with a neem lotion. For individual ulcers, apply neem leaf extract or damp whole leaves to the skin ulcer and cover with a gauze bandage overnight or until it is healed. Replace the bandage and extract daily. Drink two neem leaf teas daily for three days in severe cases.

Warts

Warts are harmless but contagious growths on the skin or mucous membranes. They infect the topmost layer of the skin and do not have roots. Warts are caused by any of the thirty types of papillomavirus. Removal typically involves either freezing or corroding acid but neem can prevent the virus from replicating and can cause the growth to slowly fade away. Neem also keeps the viruses from infecting cells and spreading new warts.

To treat the wart, cover it with whole neem leaves or soak the gauze portion of a small bandage with neem leaf extract or a neem based cream and place it over the wart. Change the bandage and reapply daily. After a week, check the area to determine the progress of the treatment.

Periodontal Diseases

Teeth and their supporting structure, the gums (gingiva) are subject to infection by streptococcus bacteria that cause cavities and pyorrhea which, if left untreated, can eventually lead to gingivitis. The bacteria adhere to the surface of the tooth and form colonies called plaque that becomes home to other bacteria. These bacteria use sugars and produce an acid that dissolves the tooth surface. This creates cavities and can eat through to the pulp, causing the pain of a toothache. If the bacteria reaches below the gum line, the infection creates the bleeding gums of gingivitis that leads to tooth loss or requires painful surgery to correct.

In a study to determine the most effective method for reducing plaque formation and the level of bacteria on tooth surfaces researchers compared antibiotics to a number of plant materials with known antibacterial properties, including neem. They found that microorganisms found in inflamed gums are resistant to penicillin (44%) and tetracycline (30%) but were not resistant to antibacterial plant extracts like neem. And unlike antibiotics, antibacterial plant extracts produced no allergy in the gingiva that could inhibit their effectiveness.

When a recent study examined neem chewing sticks for their effectiveness they proved to have both anti-plaque and antibacterial properties. The extracts of the chewing sticks were also found to be very effective in killing Strep mutans and Strep faecalis (Almas, 1999).

In a follow-up clinical study fifty patients with confirmed gingivitis were selected, forty of whom had shown severe bleeding and pustular discharges from the gums. After just three weeks of brushing twice a day with a paste that included leaf extracts, 80% showed significant improvement. The patients also showed a 50% reduction in bacterial populations and elimination of halitosis (bad breath) with no side effects (Patel and Venkatakrishna, 1998).

Neem has been used in India and all of south Asia for thousands of years as the preferred method for maintaining healthy teeth and gums. The people of India chew a neem twig until the end becomes bristles then brush with the natural "toothbrush" to clean their teeth after meals. The bark and sap within the twig help clean the teeth and protect the mouth from disease. For those not inclined to chew neem twigs, toothpastes and mouthwashes containing neem are now available. Neem toothpastes and mouthwashes prevent cavities, heal gum diseases and rejuvenate the tissues of the mouth, verifying the Ayurvedic practice of prescribing neem for dental care (Lorenz, 1976).

Pyorrhea

Pyorrhea is characterized by an inflammation of the gums and membranes that cover the roots of the teeth. More teeth are lost by people over age 35 because of this disease than any other cause. In a German study of 70 patients with pyorrhea of varying stages, after just 5 to 10 treatments with a neem-based toothpaste and mouthwash there was significant improvement. Bleeding gums had healed and the secretion from pockets around the teeth had stopped. The blue-tinted colored gums returned to a healthy pale pink color (Zeppenfeldt, undated). Neem bark is more active than the leaves against certain bacteria and is considerably less bitter, making it the neem ingredient of choice in toothpastes and mouthwashes (Vashi and Patel, 1988).

Brushing with a neem bark powder or toothpaste is recommended for mild cases or as a preventive. For advanced cases place neem bark powder over the gums and let set for thirty minutes every evening before bed.

Gingivitis (bleeding gums)

Neem bark extracts can reduce the ability of some streptococci to colonize tooth surfaces (Wolinsky *et al*, 1996), (Patel and Venkatakrishna, 1988). Gingivitis has been prevented or even reversed with regular use of neem toothpaste and mouthwash (Elvin-Lewis, 1980). One person even reported a reversal of the loss of gum tissue by chewing fresh neem leaves. Scientists believe that antibacterial compounds and neem's ability to improve the immune response in the gums and tissues of the mouth account for these results.

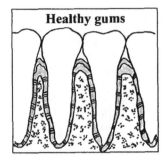
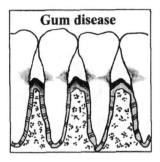

Brushing with neem toothpaste after every meal and using a mouthwash with neem extract is recommended treatment for preventing and correcting gingivitis. For severe cases also drink neem tea daily for one week.

Cavities

Cavities are caused primarily by plaque, a sticky substance formed on teeth that is made up of food remains, saliva by-products and bacteria. The acid formed by the bacteria as it breaks down the food remains gradually eats away at the tooth enamel forming a cavity.

Brushing with neem twigs has helped millions of people in south Asia avoid cavities despite a very limited access to modern dental care. With available modern preparations many people are now using commercial products that contain the same basic neem compounds.

Regular brushing with neem toothpaste and rinsing with neem mouthwash destroys cavity-causing bacteria, enhances the mouth immunity and prevents tartar and plaque buildup.

Toothache

Neem's pain-relieving compounds will temporarily reduce the discomfort of a toothache. The vasodilation and anti-inflammatory compounds will reduce the pressure on nerves that can cause the toothache.

To reduce the pain and inflammation, put a few drops of neem leaf extract and one clove on the gums near the site of the pain.

Circulatory Disorders

High blood pressure, blood clots, high cholesterol levels and arrhythmic heart action are major causes of heart attack. Neem leaf extracts have been shown to reduce clotting, lower blood pressure and cholesterol, slow rapid heartbeat, and inhibit irregularities of the rhythms of the heart. There are also reports that some compounds can produce effects similar to mild sedatives (Debelmas and Hache, 1976) reducing anxiety and other emotional and physical states that can precipitate heart attacks. This may be a calming effect similar to that witnessed with other herbal teas or a psychological result of physiological effects of blood vessel dilation and lower blood pressure.

High blood pressure

The antihistamine properties of nimbidin in leaf extracts cause blood vessels to dilate and may be responsible for reducing blood pressure (Thompson and Anderson, 1978), (Pillai and Santhakumari, 1984c). Alcoholic extract of neem leaf (intravenous) produced a significant and immediate decrease in blood pressure that lasted for several hours (Koley and Lal, 1994). The same type of extract given orally was able to produce a dose-dependent hypotensive effect without changing the amplitude or the rate of respiration (Chattopadhyay, 1997). Another neem leaf extract, sodium nimbidinate, administered to people with congestive cardiac failure, acted successfully as a diuretic (Mitra and Misra, 1967), (Bhide *et al*, 1958b), (Shah *et al*, 1958).

Drinking a cup of neem leaf tea several times a week may promote lower blood pressure via these mechanisms.

Blood clots

Neem compounds, primarily the prostaglandin inhibitors, can reduce blood clotting that often close blood vessels and cause heart attacks.

> *Occasional prophylactic use of neem tea may help keep the blood free of excessive clotting.*

Cholesterol

Neem leaf extracts reduced cholesterol levels significantly in recent studies. Alcoholic extract of neem leaves reduced serum cholesterol by about 30% beginning two hours after administration and kept the level low for an additional four hours until the test ended. (Chattopadhyay *et al*, 1992).

> *Since neem is a safe herb when used in low doses, drinking neem tea for a month to stabilize cholesterol levels may be recommended. For those that would only need small reductions, or after eating an exceptionally fatty meal, neem tea may be an alternative.*

Arrhythmia/rapid heartbeat

Neem leaf extract exhibited anti-arrhythmic activity, returning the heart to a normal rhythm within eight minutes of administration when tested with an artificially induced arrhythmia. Neem extracts can also decrease abnormally high heart rates (Thompson and Anderson, 1978).

> *Neem leaf tea several times a week may inhibit irregular heartbeats and help maintain normal heart rates.*

Poor circulation

Neem leaf extracts can cause the blood vessels to dilate, (Thompson and Anderson, 1978) allowing for increased circulation to the extremities.

Ingesting neem leaf extracts several times a week will enhance poor circulation and oxidize the blood.

Blood poisoning

Caused by bacterial infections that have infected the blood, blood poisoning is relieved by neem's anti-bacterial compounds (Patel and Trivedi, 1962). Neem has been a major blood tonic and blood purifier in the systems of medicine found in India and Pakistan. In an analysis of 36 plant drugs attributed with blood purifying properties, neem was found to have the widest range of beneficial effects (Vohora, 1986). It is believed to remove toxins from the blood and promote a healthy circulation (Chattopadhyay *et al*, 1992a). Small amounts of neem leaf extracts have been found to protect the liver from damage when toxic agents were used to induce hepatocellular necrosis (Chattopadhyay *et al*, 1992b). In a study published in 2000, aqueous neem leaf extracts (neem tea) counteracted the effects of induced liver damage at both the biochemical level and the cellular level (Bhanwra *et al*, 2000). Neem can also oxidize the blood to promote healing (Etkin, 1981).

Either whole neem leaf or teas made from neem leaves will provide the necessary neem extracts to the body.

Kidney problems

As guardians of the blood's purity, kidneys filter out the body's toxins. When filtering out tremendous amounts of these toxins after an illness, the kidneys can become overworked. They can also be adversely affected by high blood pressure and infections in the blood.

To prevent kidney problems, drink neem tea or take neem leaf capsules with barley water at the onset of infection or for high blood pressure. This helps the body fight infections and lowers blood pressure, allowing the kidneys to perform under less stress.

Digestive Disorders

Digestive disorders include conditions that disrupt the digestive process by obstruction or interfere with the breakdown or absorption of nutrients. They also include conditions that simply cause distress such as heartburn, abdominal pain or diarrhea.

Neem is a generally accepted in the Ayurvedic medical tradition as a therapy for ulcers and other types of gastric discomfort. People throughout the Indian subcontinent routinely take neem leaves for relief of stomach problems of any sort. Scientific validation of these practices is consistent in studies of the effectiveness of neem and neem extracts for gastric relief. Neem promotes a healthy digestive system by protecting the stomach, aiding in elimination and removing toxins and harmful bacteria.

Heartburn/indigestion

Neem leaves are often used to treat heartburn and indigestion. They are effective because some neem extracts reduce the concentration of hydrochloric acid in the stomach. Other compounds with apparent prostaglandin inhibition capabilities may also play a part in reducing gastric secretions.

At the onset of indigestion traditional Ayurvedic practice is to drink a strong neem tea made with five neem leaves along with 1/4 teaspoon each of ginger and baking soda. The mixture is said to protect the stomach and reduce discomfort.

Peptic/duodenal ulcers

Raw areas in the gastrointestinal tract, when bathed in acidic gastric juice, cause discomfort and can lead to severe problems if not alleviated. The discovery that many gastric ulcers were caused by the bacteria *Helicobacter pylori* raging uncontrolled in sections of the gastrointestinal tract provided a new understanding of the causes and potential cure for this condition.

Compounds in neem have been proven to have anti-ulcerative effects (Garg and Bhakuni, 1984), (Garg *et al*, 1991), (Pillai *et al*, 1978a), (Pillai *et al*, 1984a, 1984b). Oral doses of neem leaf extracts gave significant protection against peptic ulcers, duodenal ulcers and enhanced the healing process of gastric lesions (Garg *et al*, 1993). Nimbidin from seed extracts taken orally prevented duodenal lesions and peptic ulcers caused by aspirin, stress, histamine and other causes. They provided significant reductions in acid output and peptic activity of gastric fluids. The effects were most pronounced when doses were low (20 to 40 mg/kg) and increased dosages actually reduced the effectiveness of neem's anti-ulcerative effects (Pillai *et al*, 1978a), (Pillai *et al*, 1980). Neem seed extracts also showed significant healing effects from this compound for existing lesions. Similar compounds have been found in leaf extracts in lesser concentrations. Neem's antibacterial properties can also help eliminate the bacteria that cause ulcers.

Drinking neem tea or whole leaves will protect the stomach and reduce the discomfort. To heal the lesions and ulcers, a thirty-day regimen must be followed. Between meals, drink a cup of neem tea along with one teaspoon of a bismuth containing product usually used for indigestion.

Gastritis

Producing many of the same symptoms as gastric ulcers, gastritis is the inflammation of the mucous membrane lining the stomach. It is usually caused by aspirin, alcohol and *Campylobacter* bacteria. Neem extracts reduce the concentration of acid in the stomach (Garg *et al*, 1993) and have antibacterial and anti-inflammatory properties that can provide relief from the effects of gastritis.

As needed, drink neem tea or ingest neem leaves to protect the stomach and reduce discomfort.

Diarrhea

Diarrhea can be caused by allergens, viruses, bacteria or stress, among others. Neem's antibacterial, antiviral and stress reducing properties indicate its ability to treat many causes of this condition.

Hemorrhoids

In the Ayurvedic tradition as well as tribal lore of the Uttar Pradesh region of Tibet and Nepal neem is the recommended treatment for hemorrhoids (Singh, 1988). Neem helps avoid hemorrhoids by soothing the bowel and avoiding constipation by promoting elimination of waste.

If hemorrhoids already exist, neem cream or extract of neem bark applied topically to external hemorrhoids becomes a soothing and lubricating salve that also helps control bleeding and itching. It provides the anti-bacterial, anti-inflammatory and pain-relieving properties desirable when treating hemorrhoids. During flare-ups, daily doses of neem tea twice a day will work their way through the digestive system to help avoid constipation and help reduce internal hemorrhoids.

Nervous Disorders

One hour after taking aqueous leaf extracts – or neem tea – weak excitation and increased activity are seen, while decreased activity and lower muscular tone occur after five hours (Debelmas and Hache, 1976). Nimbidin has a mild suppressive effect on the central nervous system (Pillai and Santhakumari, 1984b). Neem leaf extracts have shown to produce lower activity, respiratory rate and muscle tone passivity as well as dose-dependent hypothermia (Gandhi *et al*, 1988), (Singh *et al*, 1987). The active compounds may be limonoids, because most seem to be able to pass the blood-brain barrier.

Stress

Stressful situations cause the body to produce epinephrine and cortisol hormones. These in turn produce increased heart rate, blood pressure and an overall increase in the body's metabolism. When this condition persists beyond a fairly limited time period stress reduces a persons' ability to cope with normal activities. It can also lead to depression, heart palpitations, and muscular aches.

One of the most recent discoveries for neem revealed that extracts of neem leaves have been able to reduce anxiety and stress when ingested in small quantities. In an experiment to see what, if any, effect neem leaf extract had on anxiety and stress fresh neem leaves were crushed and the liquid squeezed out to obtain a leaf extract. The extract was then given orally to test animals that were placed in two different standard stress tests and the behavior noted. As controls and for comparison three main sets of animals were used. One group received salt water to act as a base control, another group received diazepam (Valium) and another set received the neem leaf extract. To determine if neem leaf extract worked differently at different amounts the neem extract group was subdivided into sets that received ever-larger doses.

Stress can frequently produce a negative effect on the immune system. Standard anti-stress agents were tested against the ability of neem to reduce stress and neem was more effective. It not only reduced the stress indicators but almost normalized stress induced changes in the immune system (Koner *et al*, 1997).

In the elevated plus maze test doses of neem leaf extract up to 200 mg/kg showed significant anti-anxiety activity equal to or greater than diazepam. In the open field test doses of neem leaf extract up to 100 mg/kg were equal to diazepam in its anti-anxiety effect. At levels higher than 200 mg/kg and 100 mg/kg respectively the neem extract performed less well as the dosages increased until at 800 mg/kg the effect totally disappeared. The explanation for neem's anti-anxiety effect may rest with its ability to increase the amount of serotonin in the brain (Jaiswal *et al*, 1994), (Banerjee and Rembold, 1992).

The amazing part of the experiment isn't that neem can reduce anxiety. That is something that had been reported many times before scientific experimentation finally quantified it. The amazing part is that neem extracts will only work in small doses. This unique quality of neem could make neem extract a safer alternative than drugs currently used for stress that compound their effects with higher doses up to a point where they can become dangerous.

A warm neem tea can produce a calming effect by relieving the symptoms of stress; rapid heart rate, elevated blood pressure and increased metabolism. Neem reduces rapid heart rates, reduces blood pressure and relaxes tense muscles.

Insomnia

Depression and stress are major causes of insomnia. Approximately 90 percent of depressed patients have some form of sleep abnormality, and 50 to 95 percent of depressed patients complain of severely disturbed sleep. Neem has been proven to reduce stress and relax muscles, producing an effect conducive to sleep. Nimbidin, a neem leaf extract, has been shown to help initiate sleep up to 74% faster than the control group (Pillai *et al*, 1984).

A warm neem tea shortly before bedtime should produce a calming effect conducive to sleep.

Pain

Inhibition of prostaglandin synthetase by limonoids (and/or polysaccharides) reduces perceived pain. Neem leaf and bark extracts have been shown to be a more potent inhibitor of prostaglandin synthetase than acetylsalicylic acid (aspirin) and pethidine hydrochloride (Okpako, 1977), (Pillai *et al*, 1978a, 1978b), (Tandan *et al*, 1990). In some cases neem was effective at reducing pain for a significantly longer period than standard agents. Neem also reduces the activity of the central nervous system, which also reduces perceived pain (Debelmas and

Hache, 1976). According to a study led by N. Khanna, neem produces an analgesic effect upon the central and peripheral neural pathways. He also feels that both opioid and non-opioid receptors can be affected by neem (Khanna *et al*, 1995).

Drinking a strong neem leaf tea (ten leaves per cup) twice per day when the pain is strong will provide relief. The other neem compounds will act to strengthen and heal the body thereby working to remove the cause and not just the symptom.

Headache

Headaches are the result of tension, pressure or stretching of the outer linings of the brain and from the scalps' blood vessels and muscles. They are caused by many factors such as nervous tension, food allergies, hangovers and toothaches. To relieve the pain of a headache the first thing to do is to relax and try to lie down, free of distractions, along with taking a mild pain reliever. Neem contains compounds similar to aspirin (prostaglandin inhibitors) (Okpako, 1977), (Pillai *et al*, 1978b) for the relief of pain. Neem also helps reduce blood pressure and open constricted blood vessels, (Thompson and Anderson, 1978) often the cause of headaches including migraines.

Traditionally, ingesting one or two neem leaves or a tea made with the leaves is recommended for relief of both minor and migraine headaches.

Epilepsy

Seizures are abnormal electrical activity and are symptoms of a dysfunction of the brain. They can be the result of head injury, brain infections, tumors, strokes or metabolic imbalances in the body. Infectious diseases, fevers, fatigue and stress can lower the seizure threshold in epileptics. Neem leaves may help control epilepsy (Larson, 1993). A Philadelphia doctor has reported that a patient with uncontrollable epilepsy ate neem leaves for 30 days and suffered no serious attacks over the next five months. These results may be due to neem's calming effects on the central nervous system or its ability to increase blood flow through vasodilation (Pillai and Santhakumari, 1984c).

Ayurvedic practitioners recommend eating a few dried neem leaves daily to help control seizures. Leaf extracts or teas will substitute if whole leaves are unavailable.

Hives (Urticaria)

Usually associated with antigens, hives may also be caused by stress. Histamine is then released from skin cells causing fluid to leak into the skin tissue. Neem's antihistamine compounds and other compounds that calm the central nervous system treat hives in both situations.

Topical application of a neem-based cream is recommended, supplemented with neem tea twice a day if there is no immediate reduction.

Parasites

Historically, neem has been used to rid the body of all forms of parasites. Scientists have since proved that neem quickly kills external parasites and may kill internal parasites as well (Singh *et al*, 1979), (Obaseki and Jegede-Fadunsin, 1986), (Rochanakij *et al*, 1985). There are numerous Ayurvedic preparations and home remedies using neem for this purpose throughout India. In fact, simple water extracts of neem leaves are preferred over standard treatments for lice and scabies.

Lice

The head louse, body louse and crab louse all thrive on humans. All of these lice can cause considerable skin irritation as they crawl around and feed on human blood. Diseases such as relapsing fever, impetigo, trench fever and typhus have been transmitted by lice though U.S health officials believe they are only "repugnant", not serious health risks. Lice infestation is only surpassed by the common cold in frequency of childhood communicable conditions, up to 20 million per year, with treatment costs of almost $400 million per year.

Most treatments involve contact poisons that kill most of the lice but need to be repeated in 10 days to kill newly hatched lice that remained in the nits (eggs) that were unaffected. Treatment failure is being noticed more frequently as the lice develop resistance to the poisons. Instead, people try more frequent and harsher treatments to kill the lice resulting in seizures, tremors, tingling nerves, respiratory problems, burning, itching and other symptoms.

A safe alternative is neem. Neem extracts have hormone mimics that interfere with the life cycle of parasites, inhibit their ability to feed and prevent the eggs from hatching.

Lice are usually treated with shampoos incorporating neem extracts followed by applying a neem-based cream to the hair and scalp. This is left overnight and washed out in the morning. Before and after washing (with a neem based shampoo), use a flea comb to remove the dead lice and sterile eggs. Since neem is safe and does not rely on poisons to kill lice it may be used daily without fear to prevent lice infestations.

Scabies

Caused by the itch mite (*Sarcoptes scabiei*) scabies is a highly infectious skin disease, easily contracted by skin-to-skin contact. Intense itching results as the mites burrow into the skin where they lay their eggs. Contact poisons of the same type as for lice are the usual treatment with the same resulting problems.

Itch mites are affected the same way lice are affected by neem (Larson, 1993). In a test of 814 people with scabies a mixture of neem and tumeric cured 97% of the infected patients in 3 to 15 days (Charles and Charles, 1992). In another test, alcoholic extract of dried neem leaves mixed with a carrier lotion that was then spread on the affected skin completely cured all patients tested in just three days. Previous treatments of these patients with benzyl benzoate and sulpha drugs had failed to cure these same patients (Singh *et al*, 1980).

Since scabies usually affects large areas of the skin, however, soaking in warm bath water with neem leaf tincture added is recommended. After soaking in the water for about fifteen minutes, a neem soap and shampoo should be used to wash thoroughly. After the bath, a neem-based cream or lotion should be applied. The itching should be relieved immediately and the scabies eliminated in a few days. As the mites can infect bedding and clothes, all contaminated clothing should be washed with a neem soap in very hot water.

Intestinal worms

Pinworm - Humans are practically the only hosts of pinworm (*E. vermicularis*), the most common intestinal parasite seen among children in the United States. It is estimated that between 15 and 40 percent of all children are affected at some time during the first 12 years of life. Although children are particularly likely to be affected, adults sometimes harbor the parasites, especially if the children in the household have pinworms. Living in the rectum of humans, female pinworms leave the intestines through the anus and deposit eggs on the surrounding skin causing itching around the anus and disturbed sleep.

Dog roundworm - Toxocariasis is caused by larvae of *Toxocara canis* and less frequently of *T. cati* (cat roundworm), two nematode parasites of animals. Most people never realize they have been infected since rarely do symptoms appear. Infection occurs mostly in preschool children because they play in dirt frequented by pets. After infection the larvae invade the liver, heart, lungs, brain, muscle and cause various symptoms including fever, anorexia, weight loss, cough, wheezing and rashes. Only rarely does someone die from infection and then only if the heart, arteries or nervous system is attacked.

Whip worm ‑ Usually showing no symptoms, heavy infections of whip worm (*Ascaris lumbricoides*), especially in small children, can cause gastrointestinal problems (abdominal pain, diarrhea, rectal prolapse) and possibly growth retardation. Whip worm is the largest nematode parasitizing the human intestine.

Neem teas are recognized in Ayurveda as an anthelmintic (kills intestinal worms) and are regularly used throughout the tropics to rid the body of intestinal worms (Singh *et al*, 1980). There have been conflicting studies as to its effectiveness, but few who use neem for intestinal worms doubt the efficacy of neem.

Neem leaf teas twice per day for one week is the usual method for eliminating these parasites from the body. For childhood pinworms apply neem oil to the anal opening for relief from itching.

Chagas disease

The protozoan parasite, *Trypanosoma cruzi*, causes Chagas' disease, a disease that can be transmitted to humans by blood sucking "kissing bugs". Called the "South American sleeping sickness", it occurs mainly in poor, rural areas of Central and South America but has been found from the southern United States to southern Argentina. Chronic Chagas' disease is a major health problem in many Latin American countries. It is estimated that 16-18 million people are infected with Chagas disease; of those infected, 50,000 will die each year. With increased population movements, the possibility of transmission by blood transfusion has become more substantial in the United States.

The disease may not even be noticed for years or even decades after initial infection. Most people do not have symptoms until the chronic stage of infection, 10-20 years after first being infected. Its symptoms include heart disease; enlargement of the esophagus and colon; weight loss; and infection of the heart muscle. Chronic Chagas' disease and its complications can be fatal and there is no cure and treatments available are not completely effective and have side effects.

Neem extracts prevent the deadly Chagas disease (Beard, 1989) by preventing the parasite that causes it from surviving in its host, the biting "kissing bug". A single dose of azadirachtin given to the "kissing bug" provided permanent resistance to the parasite *T. cruzi*, thereby preventing transmission to humans (Gonzales and Garcia, 1992). By inoculating the "kissing bug" against infection by the parasite instead of simply poisoning the host, a buildup of resistance is reduced.

Neem leaf or seed extracts sprayed throughout the home where the kissing bug lives eliminate the parasite and prevents the kissing bug from laying eggs. Drinking neem teas may also prevent infection by transferring neem extract to the bug as they take blood.

Malaria

Malaria affects hundreds of millions of people worldwide and kills over two million people every year. It has even made an occasional appearance in North America due to the introduction of new mosquito strains and travelers from malarial regions. Malaria is transmitted from an infected person to a non-infected person by the bites of certain species of mosquito. The malarial gamete is sucked up from the infected person by the mosquito and carried in its gut until the mosquito bites an uninfected person. The bite injects the gamete into the blood stream where it travels to the kidney to mature. Neem can block the development of the gamete in an infected per-

Adult

Mosquito Life Cycle

Eggs

Pupa

Larva

son. This not only prevents the infected person from developing malaria but also stops the disease from spreading (Jones *et al*, 1994).

Neem leaf extract substantially increases the state of oxidation in red blood cells, preventing normal development of the malaria plasmodia (Etkin, 1981). An active ingredient in neem leaves, called Irodin A, is toxic to resistant strains of malaria, with 100 percent of the plasmodia dead in 72 hours with only a 1:20,000 ratio of active ingredients (Abatan and Makinde, 1986). In other experiments alcoholic extracts of neem leaf performed almost as well as the more refined compounds (Badam *et al*, 1987).

Two other compounds found in neem leaves called gedunin, a limonoid, and quercetin, a flavonoid, are at least as effective as quinine and chloroquine against malaria (Badam *et al*, 1987), (Ekanem, 1978), (Iwu *et al*, 1986), (Khalid *et al*, 1989a, 1989b), (Obaseki and Jegede-Fadunsin, 1986), (Rochanakij *et al*, 1985). Another molecule, gedunin, an extract of neem bark and neem leaves, has also been found to be effective in treating malaria (Khalid *et al*, 1989a, 1989b). When neem leaf extract was compared to 22 extracts of related species the neem extract, gedunin, was by far the most effective against Plasmodium falciparum. It was even more effective than the standard treatment of chloroquine (MacKinnon *et al*, 1997).

Several other studies show that neem extracts are effective against chloroquine-resistant strains of the malaria parasite (Obih and Makinde, 1985), (Bray *et al*, 1990). Neem seed extracts have been tested and highly purified compounds have proven to be more effective than any other anti-malaria treatment. That the compounds were effective against strains of the disease that are resistant to other drugs suggests a possible alternate mode of action. In addition, these compounds were effective not only against the parasitic stages that cause the infection but also against the stages responsible for continued malaria transmission (Dhar *et al*, 1998).

The antimalarial effects of neem appear to be greater in the body than on a petri dish. This has led some to speculate that stimulation of the immune system is a major factor in neem's effectiveness against malaria (Obaseki and Jegede-Fadunsin, 1986). Neem also lowers the fever and increases the appetite thereby strengthening the body that aids in fighting the disease parasite and speeding recovery (Abatan and Makinde, 1986).

Like the populations in malaria-stricken areas who have access to neem, some westerners familiar with neem often substitute an occasional neem leaf tea instead of drinking quinine on trips to malaria-infested areas of Africa and India as a preventive measure (Larson, 1993).

Using an insect repellent like neem to keep disease-carrying mosquitoes away is the first line of defense against malaria. Whenever traveling in areas where malaria is possible always cover exposed skin with a neem based repellent. Because of the seriousness of this disease combining Deet at a total concentration of two percent will enhance the repellency beyond either product by itself.

Drinking neem teas or simply chewing a couple of neem leaves a day reduces the possibility of contracting malaria. Even though neem tea may be effective against malaria, a study done by Dr. Udeinya showed that water extracts are less effective than leaf extracts obtained by a water/acetone combination (Udeinya, 1993). But these purified extracts are difficult to obtain and good results with water extracts means that this simple method can be effective.

Encephalitis

Simply an inflammation of the brain, encephalitis is usually caused by a virus. Mosquito borne diseases such as St. Louis encephalitis and recently West Nile encephalitis can sometimes cause death though many infected persons show little or no symptoms. Treatments are currently ineffective with antiviral medications providing only occasional relief.

Keeping the infected mosquito away from you is the best way of avoiding the disease. Neem oil is an effective repellent with none of the drawbacks of DEET. As a preventive neem can also work internally. An outbreak of Japanese encephalitis in India was apparently ended when children were dosed twice a day with crushed neem leaves (Larson, 1993).

Many diseases are carried by mosquitoes. Neem oil can also be used to kill mosquitoes before they hatch and can begin spreading their diseases. When neem oil and purified fractions of neem oil are sprayed on areas where mosquitoes breed there are a series of effects on them. In many species the larvae are prevented from maturing. In some the larvae are prevented from feeding and soon die. In still others the mosquitoes lay few eggs or the eggs laid fail to hatch (Su and Mulla, 1998), (Batra *et al*, 1998). Neem can therefore be used effectively to keep mosquito numbers down, prevent those that are around from biting and in cases where they transmit diseases neem can treat the diseases.

For external protection from the disease carrying mosquitoes apply a neem-based insect repellent or a cream with at least two-percent neem oil to exposed areas of the skin. Reapply after heavy perspiration. For internal protection during the outbreak drink a mild neem tea once per day to strengthen the immune system and provide the body with anti-viral compounds.

Neem and the Immune System

Immune system

Neem, especially neem bark, is recognized for its immunomodulatory polysaccharide compounds (Njiro and Kofi-Tsekpo, 1999). These compounds appear to increase antibody production (Chiaki *et al*, 1987), (Kores *et al*, 1993). Other compounds in neem enhance the immune system via a different mechanism; the cell-mediated immune response, (Upadhyay *et al*, 1992), (Upadhyay *et al*, 1993a), (Sen *et al*, 1993) the body's first form of defense. Only when this system appears to be unable to stop an infectious onslaught is the more massive immune system involved (Beardsley, 1992).

Powdered neem leaves were fed to chickens that had reduced immune responses after surviving bursal disease to determine if neem could stimulate their immunity. The results of the feeding showed that neem had significantly enhanced the chickens' antibodies. This indicated that neem could be beneficial in immunosuppressed conditions (Sadekar *et al*, 1998).

Neem oil acts as a non-specific immunostimulant that activates the cell mediated immune response by activating macrophages and lymphocytes. This then creates an enhanced response to any future challenges by disease organisms. When neem oil was injected under the skin there was a significant increase in leukocytic cells and peritoneal macrophages showed enhanced phagocytic activity and expression of MHC class II antigens (SaiRam *et al*, 1997). Production of gamma interferon was also induced by the injection. Spleen cells showed higher lymphocyte reaction to infection but did not augment anti-TT antibody response (Upadhyay *et al*, 1992).

Water soluble neem leaf extracts, when taken orally, produced an increase in lymphomatic counts and both red and white blood cells as well as lymphocyte counts (Prasad *et al*, 1994). In studies on the birth control effects of neem the major factor in that effect appears to be an increase in the immune response where neem has been applied that causes the body to reject the fetus as a foreign body (Upadhyay *et al*, 1993), (Tewari *et al*, 1989), (Upadhyay *et al*, 1994), (Garg *et al*, 1994).

By enhancing the cellular immune response most pathogens can be eliminated before they cause the ill feeling associated with disease. This mechanism could also help in diseases that involve the immune system, like AIDS.

Taking neem leaf or bark powder every other day or drinking a mild neem tea will enhance antibody production and the body's cell-mediated immune response, helping to prevent infections.

General Conditions

Neem works against a wide range of diseases and chronic conditions. Most of them have not responded well to medications currently available. Though not a panacea, neem can be a major factor in preventing and treating these problems, some of which have been successfully treated with neem for centuries. Prescription medicines made from neem extracts, approved by the Indian equivalent of the FDA, are used to treat a number of these conditions.

Diabetes

Diabetes is an incurable, chronic metabolic disorder that develops when the pancreas can no longer produce sufficient insulin. Blood sugar levels rapidly elevate yet the body is unable to use the energy contained in the sugar, leading to weakness and eventually unconsciousness. Diabetes is the leading cause of blindness in people ages 25 to 74. It damages nerves, kidneys, the heart and blood vessels and may result in the amputation of limbs.

Neem leaf is a traditional herb for treating diabetes (Alam, et al, 1989) and has been scientifically proven effective in treating and preventing diabetes (Murty *et al*, 1978), (Chakrabarty, 1984a, 1984b), (El-Harwary *et al*, 1990). Neem leaf was compared to other plants with historical use as blood sugar lowering medicinals and proved to have the most potent activity (Chattopadhyay, 1999).

Both the leaf and the oil have hypoglycemic properties. In tests using oral doses of neem leaf extracts there was a significant reduction of insulin requirements for non-insulin dependent diabetes (Pillai and Santhakumari, 1981b), (Luscombe and Taha, 1974), (Murty *et al*, 1978). In the tests using neem oil it was proven effective and has been able to inhibit increases in blood sugar levels by as much as 45% in test animals (Sharma *et al*, 1983), (Dixit *et al*, 1986).

Capsules containing neem and a number of other herbs are currently available in many countries for the treatment of diabetes. In tests to verify the effectiveness of the medication (Karnim) it was found blood sugar was lowered by over 50% in twenty weeks and maintained thereafter (Saraf and Joglekar, 1993). Drinking a cup of mild neem leaf tea twice daily will significantly reduce the need for insulin (Siddiqui and Mitra, 1945), (Santhoshumari and Devi, 1990).

Different studies show insulin requirement reductions of between 20 percent and 50 percent for those who take five grams of dried neem leaf capsules (Shukla *et al*, 1973). In some initial tests of the mechanism by which neem affects insulin and sucrose levels it was determined that neem leaf extracts had no action on peripheral utilization of glucose. The study also found that neem was most active against insulin inhibiting compounds when tested in diabetic rats and only slightly active in normal rats (Chattopadhyay, 1996). A more recent study by the same researcher points to a mechanism whereby neem blocks substances that can inhibit insulin secretion resulting in an increase in insulin secretions (Chattopadhyay, 1999c). All of these studies lend credence to some anecdotal reports of diabetics chewing a single neem leaf daily that have been able to eliminate insulin injections completely.

Based on the many studies of neem's effects on insulin requirements, the Indian government has approved the sale by pharmaceutical companies of neem tablets for diabetics. (Some of these preparations are really nothing more than powdered neem leaves.)

After determining an individual's tolerance to neem, the typical treatment for diabetes using neem leaf is one neem leaf capsule (.5 grams neem leaf) in the morning on an empty stomach and one after dinner.

Arthritis

Arthritis is a broad term covering many types of joint ailments. The ailments can be autoimmune disorders, infections, and the result of wear on the joints or simply inflammation. Generally, though, it is the inflammation or the pain associated with it that is treated regardless of the origin. Neem can aid in treating arthritis in many ways. Neem's antibacterial properties can help kill infectious causes while its inflammation-reducing properties and pain-suppressing properties can alleviate the symptoms. Neem can also help create a balance in the immune system that directly affects progression of the disease (Kroes *et al*, 1993).

A number of studies indicate the usefulness of neem in treating arthritis. Water extracts of neem leaf have consistently been shown to exert significant anti-inflammatory activity (Chattopadhyay, 1998). There have been numerous studies on the ability of extracts of neem leaf to reduce the inflammation caused by arthritis (Bhargava *et al*, 1970), (Okpanyi and Ezeukwa, 1981). One study suggested that the phenolic compounds containing catechin (known to possess anti-inflammatory properties) may produce the anti-inflammatory effects witnessed (Van der Nat *et al*, 1991). Another study discovered quercetin, a bioflavonoid with antioxidant, anti-inflammatory and antibacterial activity, in neem leaves (Basak and Chakraborty, 1968). Others concluded that the polysaccharides in neem reduce the inflammation and swelling associated with arthritis (Narayan, 1978), (Fujiwara *et al*, 1984), (Brahmachari and Sharma, 1958).

Different parts of the tree and many extracts of each were tested. Compounds like nimbidin, extracted from the seed with alcohol, showed significant effects against arthritis (Pillai and Santhakumari, 1981a) as have methanol extracts of the leaf and bark (Van der Nat *et al*, 1991). The reason these compounds work is believed to be due to several factors. Several leaf compounds have been shown to be more potent inhibitors of prostaglandin than aspirin (Okpako, 1977). Limonoids and catechin in the leaf and seed (Swainalakshmi *et al*, 1981), (Rao *et al*, 1983) may provide additional beneficial effects. Other possible explanations point to an inhibition of the release of mediators of acute inflammation. An antihistaminic effect of nimbidin (underlying its anti-gastric ulcer activity) has been reported (Narayan, 1969, 1978), (Pillai and Santhakumari,

1984a). Also, a modification of the immune response appears to reduce the generation of inflammation-producing chemicals (Van der Nat *et al*, 1987, 1989, 1991). In any case, the long history of using neem leaf, bark and seed extracts to relieve inflamed joints is borne out by the recent scientific investigations.

Many sufferers of arthritis are given corticosteroids as a treatment option. This is used primarily to reduce inflammation. In a study of the effects of this type of treatment on the rest of the body it was determined that significant bone loss can frequently occur in the first 12 to 24 months of treatment. This can result in osteoporosis and possible bone fractures. The effects can be countered partly with increased calcium intake and Vitamin D metabolites and, in women, estrogen replacement therapy (Sambrook, 2000). However, bone loss will be a factor whenever corticosteroids are used for any length of time. Neem has anti-inflammatory effects and does not produce bone loss.

Treatment for arthritis is traditionally a mild neem leaf tea coupled with rubbing a warmed neem-based cream on the stiff or painful areas as needed.

Rheumatism

Rheumatism is a term used for any condition that causes pain or stiffness in muscles and joints. The active constituents in neem leaves have outstanding anti-inflammatory activity, comparable even to the well-known modern drugs phenyl butazone and cortisone (Puri, 1993), (Narayan, 1978). They relieve pain by acting on the prostaglandin mechanism and significantly reducing acute paw edema (Shah *et al*, 1958), (Okpako, 1977). Topical applications of a warmed cream containing neem oil along with a mild neem tea will help alleviate the pain associated with these conditions.

Drinking a mild neem tea once a day for two weeks should produce an increased activity level as the infections dimin-

ish. Thereafter, the tea should be taken only every other day for another two weeks.

Inflammation

Taking neem leaf or neem bark orally and applying a cream containing neem oil topically has been used for centuries to reduce inflammation. A compound called sodium nimbinate found in neem leaves has been shown to provide significant relief to inflamed tissue (Okpanyi and Ezeukwa, 1981), (Lorenz, 1976). Other compounds such as nimbin, nimbinin and nimbidol are comparable to cortisone acetate in reducing inflammation (Wali *et al*, 1993), (Narayan, 1978), (Tandan *et al*, 1990). In one test with hydrocortisone, neem extract (sodium nimbinate) and several natural saponins, neem was over four times more effective at reducing inflammation than hydrocortisone and more effective than the other agents tested (Bhargava *et al*, 1970).

Topical application of a neem-based cream over the inflamed area can provide relief from the pain and from the inflammation itself. Supplementing the topical treatment with a mild neem leaf or neem bark tea will give the body compounds to reduce and help heal the cause of the inflammation.

Fatigue (chronic)

No one knows what causes chronic fatigue. There are theories that it is caused by excessive stress, rampant fungal infection or Epstein-barr viruses. Neem extracts have proven effective against both fungal and viral infections as well as an ability to relieve stress (Jaiswal *et al*, 1994), (Rao *et al*, 1969), (Thind and Dahiya, 1977). Neem also works to enhance the immune response on a cellular level so it is more effective in fighting disease-causing agents (Kroes *et al*, 1993), (Chaiki *et al*, 1987), (Upadhyay *et al*, 1990).

A mild neem leaf or neem bark tea twice per day for two weeks can help the body fight the condition. If the symptoms persist use a strong (ten leaves or two grams of leaf or neem bark) tea twice per day for three days then revert to the mild tea for four days.

Cancer

Unrestrained growth of cells of organs or tissues, cancer is a major cause of death and suffering. Herbalists throughout Southeast Asia have used the neem tree successfully for centuries to reduce tumors. Researchers in India, Europe and Japan have now found that polysaccharides and limonoids found in neem bark, flowers, leaves and seed oil reduced tumors and cancers (Fujiwara *et al*, 1982), (Chatterjee, 1961), (Hartwell, 1983), (Kusamran *et al*, 1998) and showed effectiveness against lymphocytic leukemia (Pettit *et al*, 1983). In several patents issued in Japan hot water neem bark extracts showed remarkable effectiveness against several types of tumors. (Shimizu *et al*, 1985a, 1985b). A series of extracts were tested at different doses and compared to the effectiveness of a standard anti-cancer agent. Several of the extracts were equal to or better than the standard anti-cancer agent against solid tumors. When the tests were done using a more purified extract of neem bark, the results were even more impressive against solid tumors. But the extracts tested were still very crude when compared to the extremely purified active compounds typically used in treating tumors. Further studies using truly pure active compounds are expected to produce results at least equal to the control.

In one study researchers used an extract of neem leaves to prevent the adhesion of cancer cells to other cells in the body (Udeinya, 1994). Without the ability to stick to other cells, cancers cannot spread through the body and are more easily destroyed by the body's own immune system or by other treatments. In another study neem leaves were fed to rats to determine how they affected liver enzymes. The results showed neem flowers were able to induce creation of compounds that possess chemoprotective activity, especially against chemicals that activate carcinogens (Kusamran *et al*, 1998).

In general, neem is known for its ability to effect cancers. Injections of neem extract around tumors showed remarkable reduction in size in just a few weeks. Skin cancers may be particularly responsive to neem. A number of reports have been made by patients that skin cancers have disappeared after several months of daily application of a neem-based cream.

Neem leaf extract can provide protection against cancer causing agents through its antioxidant and by promoting detoxifying enzymes (Rao *et al*, 1998). In an experiment using rats as subjects neem leaf extracts were given orally for five consecutive days to a group of rats. All of the rats were then injected with a potent cancer causing nitrosamine, which was expected to produce severe effects on enzyme levels. The scientists discovered that the neem leaf extracts enhanced the level of antioxidants and of detoxifying enzymes in the stomach, the main target of the administered carcinogen (Arivazhagan *et al*, 2000).

Ayurvedic doctors are using neem as an adjunct to standard chemotherapy in treating breast and gastrointestinal cancer. The patients are told to chew 8 to 10 neem leaves in the morning with lukewarm water on an empty stomach. The doctors have observed an increase in white blood cell counts (which normally go down with chemotherapy) (Dr. Preeti Kachroo, personal communication).

Cancer should be treated as a "whole body" disease with proper diet and mild exercise in addition to standard and natural therapies. Skin cancers can be treated with topical application of neem oil on the affected areas along with neem bark or leaf teas daily. Internal cancers would use twice daily teas for increased white cell counts and to retard the growth of the cancers. If the disease is advanced the teas could be replaced by five drops of neem oil orally by placing the oil in a vegicap just before consumption.

Bronchitis

Bronchitis, the acute inflammation of the respiratory system, is generally caused by complications of a cold or flu, but is more common among smokers or those exposed to pollution. In experiments with cattle, when neem oil is included in the feed the number of lung infections is significantly decreased when compared to a control group. Neem can reduce the inflammation and combat some of the causes of the disease such as bacteria and viruses.

Bronchitis has long been treated with a combination of oral doses of neem leaf tea twice a day along with inhaling the steam of boiled neem leaves. The steam will contain volatile oils and aromatic compounds that, when inhaled, will reduce the inflammation and attack the disease agents directly. The oral doses of neem will provide the entire body with fever-reducing and disease-fighting compounds as well as compounds that can dilate air passages.

Allergies

Allergies are exaggerated reactions of the immune system to harmless substances. A byproduct of the response is histamine, which causes the major symptoms of allergies. Neem inhibits allergic reactions when applied externally or consumed internally (Narayan, 1978). Neem compounds inhibit the stimulus produced by histamine and may be helpful in skin rashes and bronchial allergy.

Application of a neem-based cream or lotion will stop the itching and inflammation of rashes and other topical allergic reactions. For the general malaise of allergies such as aches, pains and tiredness, neem tea may be taken internally. If there are problems with air passages, neem tea mixed with inhaling the vapors of boiled neem leaves will counteract the allergies effects and help clear air passages.

Conjunctivitis

The inflammation of the eye may be caused by bacteria, viruses or allergies. Because neem is active against each of these causes it can be treated with drops of room temperature neem tea prepared from powdered neem leaves (Puri, 1993). *[Tincture should not be used due to the alcohol used in the extract.]

A few drops of the tea into each eye every three hours for two to three days should be sufficient. Overnight, a natural cream with neem oil should be wiped around the eye and eyelid.

Bad breath

The usual reason for chronic bad breath is bacteria, infections or gastric upset. The most common site of bad breath causing bacteria is the back of the tongue, where bacteria grow unregulated and produce gases by their digestive actions. The bacteria that cause bad breath can form a film that is difficult to gargle away and must be either scraped or brushed away. Once the film is removed and the bacteria are exposed neem extract will easily destroy the bacteria.

Neem toothpastes and mouthwashes contain proven antibacterial and anti-viral compounds that can stop bad breath where it originates. If the cause is infection of the mouth, brushing the teeth and gums with neem toothpaste and rinsing afterward with neem extract will kill the infection and promote healing. For bad breath caused by gastric upset, ingestion of neem leaves or fresh seed kernel is traditionally recommended to relieve the upset and correct any acid imbalance.

Hangover

The headaches, stomach upset and general ill feeling of a hangover can be relieved by neem tea. Neem "resets" the blood glucose levels, opens constricted blood vessels, reduces blood pressure, and counteracts the body's reaction to the alcohol.

Anecdotal reports seem to indicate that taking neem daily a few days in advance of a party works very well as a preventive. For relief after drinking excessive amounts of alcohol, drink a cup of hot neem tea made with ten neem leaves.

Smoking

Nimbidin has produced up to a 90% blockage of the spasmodic effect of nicotine (Pillai and Santhakumari, 1984c). Neem's calming action on the nervous system may also reduce the anxiety and desire for nicotine as well as counter the effect nicotine has on the body.

Neem extracts in the form of a tea or from ingested leaf could offer a method for reducing the effects of nicotine and enable smokers to stifle the addiction.

❧ III ❧

How Neem Works on the Biochemical Level

B ecause neem is new to Western scientists, the number of pharmacological studies on neem has been somewhat limited. In those studies that have been made, the general conclusion is that neem not only kills some infective organisms directly but also boosts the immune response on several levels. This increases the body's ability to fight bacterial, viral, and fungicidal infections itself.

This combination of effects is more effective in the long run because chemicals toxic enough to eliminate all microbes also often harms healthy body tissue and cause undesirable side-effects. An improved immune system can selectively wipe out the invading microbes without adversely affecting other cells.

When invaded by microbes (or anything else the body recognizes as foreign), the immune system releases antibodies that lock onto and neutralize the intruder. Neem not only enhances antibody production but also seems to improve the cell-mediated immune response by which white blood cells are unleashed to kill the invaders. In this type of immune response, special scavenger cells in the blood called macrophages devour the microbes and present bits of them along with their own surface molecules. It is only after macrophages (or other antigen-presenting cells) present bits of the microbe as antigens that helper T cells recognize the antigens. These helper T cells then release chemical messengers called cytokines that galvanize other cells of the immune system into a counter-attack (Upadhyay *et al*, 1990). By enhancing the body's first line of defense, neem helps the immune system more quickly respond to infections that might otherwise gain a strong foothold that would then be more difficult to overcome.

Is Neem Safe?

Historical Perspective

The first evidence about the safety of neem is its extensive use in India for at least the last four thousand years by humans and animals. The leaves are eaten by animals as forage (Kehra, 1949) while the fruit is eaten by both birds and man (Ketkar, 1976). Seed kernels and leaves are occasionally used as a bitter spice in some of the hotter Indian foods. Mahatma Gandhi regularly ate a chutney with neem leaves for general health (National Research Council, 1997). After meals many people eat one or two neem seed kernels to aid digestion and to kill bacteria in the mouth.

Neem oil has been used for illness much the way castor oil was used by mothers in America. A teaspoon was given to children for almost every complaint. (Neem tastes much worse than castor oil so children in India had to be really sick before they dared tell their mothers.) Though studies now show that this may not be a safe practice for infants and very small children, neem oil is still routinely given by mothers for a variety of illnesses.

Bathing with neem leaves in hot water is another routine practice in India. Whenever there are conditions of the skin, from allergic reactions to severe skin diseases, bathing with neem is the general practice. There has not been a report of any problems with putting neem on the skin, either oil or leaf. In fact, whenever neem is applied topically, it seems to cure just about any dermatological problem. The safety of neem applied outside the body has never been a question. For any skin disease or skin allergy, neem is considered the ultimate cure.

Toxicological Perspective

Numerous studies of possible toxicity resulted in a determination that leaf and bark are very low in toxicity, especially when taken orally (Khattak *et al*, 1985), (Sinniah and Baskaran, 1981), (Sinniah *et al,* 1983), (Uwaifo, 1984), (Pillai and Santhakumari, 1984b), (Bhargava *et al*, 1970), (Rojanapo *et al*, 1985), (Debelmas and Hache, 1976), (Singh *et al*, 1987). But large doses of neem leaves taken internally have caused some side effects in some of the animals in which it was tested (Sinniah *et al*, 1983), (Okpanyi and Ezeukwa, 1981). It appears that neither should be taken in large doses for extended periods of time.

Extensive research has been conducted on neem oil extracts for regulatory agencies in several countries, including the United States, and has been found to be safe in limited dosage for short periods of time. Tests on animals required by the Environmental Protection Agency showed that alcohol extracts of the seed produced no external irritation in rabbits and no toxic effects on mice when taken internally, even in very large amounts (Larson, 1987).

Some people taking neem oil internally experienced nausea and general discomfort (Chopra *et al*, 1965), which is the case with many of the sulpha compounds containing oils. Excessive consumption of raw neem oil has been implicated in reduced liver functioning (Thompson and Anderson, 1978), (Okpanyi and Ezeukwa, 1981), (Bhide *et al*, 1958a), (Sinniah *et al*, 1983). The toxic effects of neem oil consumption has been disputed (Rochanakij *et al*, 1985), (Larson, 1987) by some researchers that believe contamination with aflatoxin or inadvertent additions of the oil of the chinaberry tree, a related species to neem known to be toxic, is the cause of the observed side effects (Quadri *et al*, 1984), (Jongen and Koeman, 1983).

Neem oil taken orally and vaginally after intercourse has been found to possess anti-implantation and abortifacient effects. Since the oil is extremely bitter it is doubtful if anyone would choose to ingest it, but pregnant women or those trying to conceive should never ingest neem oil and should also avoid using it intra-vaginally.

There is no definitive answer regarding the toxicity of ingested neem oil, but caution should be exercised whenever taking neem oil internally. Neem oil, though consumed frequently in small doses in India, is not recommended for internal consumption until final toxicology studies are completed using neem oil prepared with the same care given to food oils, which is not currently the case. However, when an experimental amount of debittered neem oil was prepared according to WHO and FDA guidelines, the oil was determined to be safe for human consumption on a par with other seed oils (Chinnasamy *et al*, 1993).

The leaves and bark appear to be very safe to consume in reasonable quantities. However, neem has many active compounds and should be categorized with other medicinal herbs and should be used judiciously. Like any substance, there are those who will be intolerant of neem. Most people living in India have grown up with neem in their foods, as medicine and for hygiene. Some people in India eat tremendous amounts of neem leaves and frequently drink neem oil without any apparent ill effect. However, for those not as familiar with neem, it may be something that should be used judiciously until a determination can be made about the level of tolerance or intolerance, depending on the individual's body chemistry. In any case, whenever something produces undesirable effects it should be stopped or the level of use reduced. This holds true for neem as with any other substance.

Comparative Toxicity of Common Chemicals

Common chemical name	LD50 mg/kg	LD50 ounces per 150 lb. person
Nicotine sulfate	50-55	0.1
Sevin	246-283	0.6
aspirin	1200	2.8
Rotenone or Pyrethrin	1500	3.6
Malathion	2800	6.7
Table salt	33200	8
Sabadilla	5000	12
Neem	7500	18

Graph Courtesy of Allen Jobes, Kerr Center for Sustainable Agriculture

❧ IV ❧

Major Active Constituents

Figuring out exactly how an herb works and which compound or combination of compounds are making it work is difficult. Constituting possibly hundreds of compounds, some active and others not, herbs are usually analyzed for their most active compound. This is done by systematically isolating each compound and determining its structure. This can show the class of chemical it belongs to and can indicate what type of effect it can be expected to have. With complex molecules, this process is very time-consuming, very expensive and often frustrating.

Neem trees have many unique compounds that have been identified and others that are as yet unidentified. The more common and therefore the most analyzed compounds are as follows:

nimbin - anti-inflammatory, anti-pyretic, antihistamine, anti-fungal

nimbidin - antibacterial, anti-ulcer, analgesic, anti-arrhythmic, anti-fungal

nimbidol - antitubercular, anti-protozoan, anti-pyretic

gedunin - vasodilator, anti-malaria, anti-fungal

sodium nimbinate - diuretic, spermicide, anti-arthritic

quercetin - anti-protozoal, antioxidant, anti-inflammatory and antibacterial

salannin - repellent

azadirachtin - repellent, anti-feedant, anti-hormonal

Neem Leaves

Neem leaves are about 20 percent fiber, 50 percent carbohydrates, 15 percent proteins, 5 percent fat, 8 percent ash, 2 percent calcium and contain essential amino acids (Keher and Nagi, 1949), (Dakshinmurthi, 1954), (Mitra and Misra, 1967). The known amino acid content of the leaf and the percentages are: alanine, 1.2; aspargine, 3.4; aspartic, 2.7; cystine, 3.3; glutamic acid, 3.1; isoleucine, 1.0; phenylaline, 3.2; proline, 2.1; threonine, 2.4; tryptophan, 1.4; taurine, .7; and valine, 2.9. There are reports that neem leaf also contains carotene and ascorbic acid (Tirimanna, 1984), (Bhandari and Mukerji, 1959).

NEEM LEAVES

Major concentrations of the active compounds are found in the seed and oil though most are also found in the leaf and bark but in lesser amounts. Historically, neem leaves and neem bark have been the primary neem ingredients in the ancient medicinal preparations because of their availability throughout the year and the ease of extracting the compounds as a decoction or by tinctures.

Most of the bitter active compounds are soluble in alcohol and water. Therefore, tinctures using 50 to 80 percent alcohol capture the majority of the medicinal compounds. Making a tea using hot but not boiling water will quickly capture them as well though excessive heat may damage some of the compounds.

Neem leaves should be gathered only from organic or wild trees. This will ensure the best complement of natural elements and reduce possible contamination by environmental toxins. They should be washed after harvest with pure water and dried in a dust-free environment. Grinding the dried leaves into fine powder will allow a greater surface area for the release of beneficial compounds. The fine neem powder can be used to make tincture, teas or used as a bitter spice on foods. For external use, the powder can be incorporated into cosmetics, face masks or herbal preparations.

Neem Bark

The bark of the neem tree is considered equal to the leaf in healing properties in the Ayurvedic system. It is used in many preparations to improve general health but is generally known for its marvelous powers of preventing and healing gum diseases and other dental problems. The bark is now known to possess large numbers of catechins and powerful immunomodulatory and immuno-stimulating compounds.

The bark has been found to contain 3.43% protein, 0.68% alkaloids and 4.16% minerals. The percentage amino acid composition of the total protein generally found by the research was; arginine, 0.125; aspargine, 0.375; aspartic acid, 0.280; cystine, 0.500; glutamic acid, 0.239; isoleucine, 0.057; methionine, 0.125; norleucine, 0.138; phenylaline, 0.088; proline, 0.300; tryptophan, 0.456. Some of the other important compounds reported are nimbin, nimbinin, nimbidin, nimbosterol, and a margosine bitter principal (Bhandari and Mukerji, 1959), (Vashi and Patel, 1988), (Nyak and Pattabiraman, 1978).

Some of the research done on the bark extracts has found the following interesting medicinal effects:

Polysaccharides in neem bark extracts have been found to possess anti-tumor and interferon inducing as well as anti-inflammatory activities (Van der Nat *et al,* 1991). Neem bark contains gallic acid, (+)- gallocatechin, (-) epicatechin (as a 2:1 mixture), (+)- catechin and epigallocatechin. These phenolic compounds in the bark are considered to be the active principals involved in the anti-inflammatory activity. Neem bark increased cellular immunity by the stimulation of the lymphocyte function as shown by an increase in MIF, a lymphokine which, in the body, attaches macrophages to monocytes to their sites of action (Van der Nat *et al*, 1991).

Neem Gum

Neem gum, usually obtained from wounds to the tree trunk, has a number of amino acids and a significant amount of protein. The breakdown of the amino acids provides the following in parts per thousand: Lysine, 44; histidine, 17; arginine, 27; aspartic acid, 138; threonine, 66; serine, 75; glutamic acid, 78; proline, 73; glycine, 73; alanine, 53; cystine, 18; valine, 75; methionine, 3; isoleucine, 51; leucine, 84; tyrosine, 30; phenyl-alanine, 57; glucosamine, 38 (Anderson *et al*, 1972).

Neem Oil

The neem seed kernel is very rich in fatty acids, (Skellon *et al*, 1962) often up to 50 percent of the kernel's weight. Neem seed oil is very bitter with a garlic/sulfur smell and contains vitamin E and other essential amino acids. Studies of the various components of the oil have found the percentages of the following fatty acids: oleic acid, 52.8; stearic acid, 21.4; palmitic acid, 2.6; linoleic acid, 2.1; and various lower fatty acids, 2.3 (Bhandari and Mukerji, 1959). The percentages vary from sample to sample depending on place and time of collection of the seeds.

Neem oil is an excellent moisturizing oil that contains compounds with historical and scientific validity as medicinals. Use of the oil for cosmetics and medicines has been limited by its strongly bitter taste and sulfur/garlic smell. Neem oil has usually been a dark, unpleasant smelling, bitter oil. Only when it was made into soaps was it acceptable for use by most people. It is no wonder the leaves have been substituted for the oil to get the benefits of neem.

Obtaining Quality Neem Oil

To bring the many therapeutic effects of neem oil to all the people that could benefit from them requires a major change in neem oil's quality. From the picking of the fruit to filling the oil into drums, careful attention to quality is the only way to get the best oil possible. It is now known that if the neem seed is not dried and stored properly and the oil is not expressed in a hygienic way the oil will be very dark, have a foul odor and may contain dangerous contaminants.

Methods for obtaining neem oil

The first thing to consider is the collection of the seeds. Neem is not considered a plantation tree in India so the seeds must be gathered from wild trees growing on the fringes of farms, along hillsides and from roadsides and shade trees around homes in the rural villages. Collection of the seeds is a seasonal affair that has historically been organized by cooperatives that press the oil from the seeds for soap manufacture.

TRADITIONAL NEEM OIL PRESS

As the ripe fruit falls to the ground, it is gathered from around the trees. Birds will have eaten some of the fruit and the seeds excreted. Other fruit may have been on the ground for weeks, covered with mold or simply rotten. The collected fruit is then carried to a water supply to wash away the fruit covering the seed. After washing, the seeds are set out to dry in the sun. The dry seeds are bagged and sold to village merchants who later sell them to an oil processing facility.

There are three main processes for extracting the oil from

the seed kernels with some companies using combinations. The one used since antiquity is the mechanical press method. Neem seed kernels are place into a tub and either a screw or some form of press is used to squeeze the kernels under pressure until the oil is pressed out and collected.

The second method uses steam and high pressures to extract the oil. The kernels are heated with steam to increase the oil flow then squeezed under high pressure. Most of the oil is extracted from the kernels but it is dark with an unpleasant smell and the high temperatures destroy many of the active compounds.

The third and newest method is solvent extraction. Most seed oil processors use this method since almost all of the oil is removed from the kernels. The neem seed kernels are finely ground and placed into a container along with a petroleum solvent, usually hexane (white gasoline). The neem oil is captured by the solvent and is pulled out of the kernels. The solvent/neem oil mixture is then put into a vat where the solvent is recovered leaving a relatively clear neem oil. Sometimes seed cake obtained after mechanical pressing is further extracted using this method. Many of neem oil's active compounds are not soluble in hexane and are left behind in the solvent extraction process. But many of the most pungent smelling compounds are also not in the oil, making it more usable for health and beauty aids.

Once the oil has been extracted, it is usually put into metal drums for storage and shipment. Since small manufacturers use neem oil primarily for soap manufacture, there has been no demand for pure or clean neem oil. Therefore, inexpensive second-hand drums are used to store the oil. With used drums, there is the possibility of contaminating the neem oil with dangerous chemicals that could have been previously stored in the drums. Purchasing neem oil in the open marketplace will usually provide the purchaser with very low quality oil that is potentially contaminated.

The best method for obtaining quality neem oil with a majority of the active compounds intact is cold pressed. In cold pressing the oil is lighter in color with milder odor (Ramakrishna *et al*, 1993). There is also the elimination of any potential residual solvents in the oil that could pose health hazards to the consumer. The downside is that high quality cold pressed neem oil is more expensive to produce than solvent extracted oil and is much harder to obtain. Few processors are willing to forego the loss of any of the oil that could have been extracted by solvent and have quit using cold presses.

Improved method for obtaining neem oil

Experiments with the collection, storage and extraction procedures have disclosed that the main reason the oil smelled of strong sulfur and was dark in color was the very procedures traditionally used. The seeds were often old and rancid before they were even collected. Storing the seeds in the hot, humid Indian summer made them even worse. By the time they were processed, the kernels were black and unpleasant smelling, which resulted in black, unpleasant smelling oil.

A better method requires the collection of seeds specifically for the manufacture of quality health and beauty aid products. Light green kernels from fresh seeds yield a light oil with only a slight odor and a tolerable bitter taste. To get this high-quality oil, neem fruit has to be picked from the trees rather than gathered off the ground.

The fresh fruit then has to be taken to an air conditioned facility where it is washed to remove the fruit from the seeds and the clean seeds quickly air dried in a room that is cool and has low humidity. Dried seeds are then de-husked and the kernels cold-pressed in a low pressure, low heat oil press. The kernels should only be pressed once to obtain "super virgin cold-pressed" oil, guaranteeing only the oil is removed, leaving the waxy and tar-like substances behind. The light, odor-free neem oil must then be placed in new drums that are stored inside the air-conditioned environment for later shipment to the manufacturing facility. This method produces high-quality neem oil suitable for use in any health and beauty aid product.

Secondary pressing with higher pressures and temperatures can then be used to extract the majority of the remaining oil. This oil, considerably darker and with the characteristic neem smell, could be used for making soaps or for use in insect repellents and pet care products.

COLD-PRESSED NEEM OIL COLOR AND CLARITY

*Left, Standard Quality; Center, Virgin Cold-Pressed;
Right, Super-Virgin Cold-Pressed*

Comparison to Other Herbs

There are a select few herbs that have been revered for many centuries for their curative powers. Over the ages these herbs have become critical parts of the medical tradition of the cultures that use them. Though separated by vast distances and variations in customs, the people who used these herbs found each to possess almost miraculous powers to prevent and heal illnesses long before they could begin to understand how they worked.

Depending on the plant materials available to the practitioner, the herbs used varied from culture to culture. Each culture's herbalists discovered the properties of plants that they had access to and developed their healing preparations from the available supply. Neem has not been a part of any major western herbal traditions and remains almost unique to Ayurveda.

Neem remained unique to Ayurveda and to India in part because the seeds cannot be stored and because neem survives only in tropical climates. Wherever there are below freezing temperatures, neem will not grow (unless grown in a greenhouse). This has excluded Europe and the rest of the nontropical regions from growing neem trees. Therefore, to most western herbalists, neem is still unknown.

Despite the tremendous advances that have been made in science and technology, a clear understanding of the mechanisms that enable herbs to provide their curative actions remains elusive. In fact, after thousands of years as a mainstay in Western medicine, scientists still don't know exactly why or how aspirin (originally from willow bark) works. What can be determined is that many herbs continue to provide relief from many ailments and are used because they work. A few herbs are particularly effective for a broad range of ailments and seem to stand out above others.

Chaparral from the southwest United States, echinacea from the plains states and neem from India are each considered to be the most effective herbs from these ancient medical heritages. Each seems to impart an ability to ward off diseases, to lessen the severity of existing conditions and to heal those who use them.

COMPARISON OF HERBAL EFFICACIES

	Chaparral	Echinacea	Neem
Anti-bacterial	yes	yes	yes
Anti-fungal	yes	yes	yes
Antiseptic	yes	yes	yes
Anti-viral	yes	yes	yes
Anti-inflammatory	yes	yes	yes
Antipyretic	no	no	yes
Anti-cancer	yes	yes	yes
Analgesic	yes	no	yes

Neem in Europe and North America

Neem Products Available in Europe

A few years ago neem was almost unknown in Europe or North America though Europe had some knowledge of it, especially in England. Contacts between India and England have been established for centuries and products containing neem were imported from India regularly for the sizable south Asian populations living there. In shops catering to the Indian population the list of available neem products in England included most of the products listed earlier except for the drugs and insect control products. These have not been approved for use by the necessary regulatory agencies. The available products are from the larger manufacturers and are relatively well made.

German researchers were the first western scientists to discover the efficacy of the many compounds found in neem, starting the worldwide interest in neem. German scientists and herbalists, therefore, knew about neem and some Indian products made with neem are sold there. German researchers have patented a process to extract compounds from neem that are made into high-quality toothpastes by German manufacturers. They are popular for their proven ability to fight cavities and gum disease.

Neem Products Available in North America

In Canada, like England, there are smaller but still sizable Indian communities where people are familiar with neem and demand easy access to products containing neem. Specialty shops in Canada import neem soaps, toothpastes, mouthwashes and shampoos from India to satisfy that need. Canadians can find a variety of products containing neem made in India and a few shops carry the German toothpastes.

In the United States, the Indian communities are smaller and more dispersed than in England or Canada. Some products containing neem could be found in isolated specialty shops but the selection was usually limited to bar soaps. For those who wanted larger selections of neem products, relatives and friends still in India were often asked to send packages from home.

There were and still are few references on neem in books dealing with natural healing, encyclopedias or dictionaries in the United States although stories of the "miracle tree from India" can be found in some newspapers, science magazines and environmental newsletters. For the most part, neem is a new and unknown herb to most people. Products made with neem that are readily available in the United States are rather limited.

The Internet has changed the availability of neem products and information about neem. There are several American companies that sell a variety of neem products on the Internet. Foreign companies, especially Indian companies, have also created a web presence for their neem products. Purchasing them is easy and safe over the Internet though delivery time, quality and reliability gives the American companies a decided edge.

With demand for neem products growing, and sales on the Internet proof of that demand, health food stores in the United States are now beginning to carry neem products though the selection is not what is available on the Internet. Stores are usually carrying only tincture and capsules with only a few carrying skin lotion and crème. The following is a list of the most commonly available neem products on the Internet. Those available in health food stores will be so noted.

Tinctures/extracts

Several companies are currently selling tinctures of neem leaves in health food stores and through the Internet. More "name brand" companies will begin selling neem extract as part of their product line as more people become aware of the benefits neem can provide and as businesses try to satisfy the demand.

Toothpastes

American-manufactured products containing neem extracts and seed oil are only now beginning to make their way to health food stores. Some neem-based toothpastes are being imported into the U.S. from India. Germany makes toothpaste using neem bark extracts but few stores carry the product.

Mouthwash

No companies are currently selling a mouthwash containing neem but one company is planning to release this product soon.

Soaps (Bar)

A few companies sell several American-made varieties of hand-made, vegetable oil bar soaps. There are a few neem-based soaps imported from India and sold primarily in specialty shops that cater to Indian and Pakistani communities.

Shampoos

Only one company is currently selling an American-made neem-based shampoo that can be found in some health food stores. A number of other companies are planning to market neem based shampoos in the near future.

Creams and lotions

Several companies sell American-made skin creams and body lotions that are available on the Internet and through health food stores. There are some creams and lotions imported from India that can be found in specialty stores.

Powdered neem leaves

At least three American companies are selling vegetarian capsules containing powdered neem leaves. An Indian company is also selling imported capsules that probably contain neem oil and leaf extract. Some health food stores carry crushed

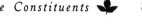

neem leaves to be used for tea or spice. Sometimes a species of Murraya, found in India, is known as "sweet neem" and confused with neem. These leaves are not bitter in taste but have a mild spicy aroma. They are used to flavor soups and curries. They do not have any of the curative properties of true neem leaves.

Medicines

There have been no medicines approved by the FDA that have neem extracts or compounds included as an ingredient. Some medicinal preparations containing neem are imported from India for application on skin diseases, as a blood purifier or for diabetes. Some of these may be found in specialty shops or over the Internet.

Insect repellents

An outdoor spray, sold by two American companies, contains neem oil and leaf extracts along with other repellent herbs and oils. They are found on the Internet and in some health food stores. Similar foreign-made products can be found on the Internet and in some specialty shops.

Pet care

There are several companies making neem-based pet care products and they are available on the Internet and in some health food stores. Several companies are planning to expand the pet-care lines to include shampoos, dips and sprays in the near future. These products are effective, natural, non-toxic alternatives for the control of pests like fleas and ticks as well as for mange and other skin diseases.

Insect control

Two American companies have both received food crop approval for their azadirachtin-rich products after extensive research and testing. Both products are marketed to commercial growers in large and very expensive gallon containers. For the home gardener, another company sells both quart containers and small individual-use tubes. Other products made from neem oil and extracts are being tested for approval against plant fungi and nematodes.

❧ V ❧

Testimonials

Acne

"I am only 13 years old and I apply the neem cream on my face before going to bed for my acne. I do this after washing with neem soap. It really works! After only two weeks my acne is gone!"

"I put neem cream on my acne at night and in the morning and the next day the acne is dried up! Something else I have noticed is that it dries up the acne without drying my skin."

C.C. – FL

Athletes foot

"I put the neem cream on my athlete's foot that was open and often bleeding. My feet were completely healed in two weeks."

Blood pressure

"I only take half the high-blood pressure medication after taking the capsules for less than a month."

Dandruff

"I used Neem oil for 2 weeks and it healed my severe case of dandruff…This was after visiting a dermatologist and using prescription lotions that worked temporarily; after using several over-the-counter shampoos; after being told by everyone that there was no cure for dandruff and after suffering with this embarrassing problem for years." – B.F. - Miami, FL

Dermatitis

"I have suffered with atopic dermatitis for over thirty years and have tried every nonprescription treatment available. After using neem lotion for six months use my skin is softer and less irritated than at any time I can remember." – T.K – FL

Dry skin

"My wife had rough, dry skin on her elbows that ordinary creams could not help. She used neem cream on her elbows and was amazed with the results. Her elbows are almost back to normal." – B.D. - Winter Park, FL

Eczema

"My 4-1/2 month old grandson has persistent eczema. One application (of neem cream) has virtually cleared it up. Everyone knows someone with this problem and I have already been asked to provide a jar for this condition." – D.P. – Canada

"I've been using neem products for about two years…I honestly don't know what I'd do without neem. I had recurring eczema on the back of my hands for years and could never get it to go completely away, even though I tried tons of different products. It itched, looked awful and drove me crazy. The only thing that helped at all was neem, which made it disappear altogether. Neem is really amazing… I always tell people how great it is, even though they probably think I'm nuts!" – L.P. - Manchester, CT

"My 14 month old baby girl suffered from eczema until I tried neem cream on her. Her skin has cleared up and is pretty as a peach!" – M.R. - Florida

"I had a small patch of eczema on my cheek that is completely gone. When I am at work I use a surgical mask and it causes a burning inflammation at the corners of my mouth. I have not had this problem since using neem soap and applying neem cream after my bath."

Heat rash

"I have a heat rash on my chest that goes away after applying neem leaf tincture after a bath."

Herpes

"When I put neem cream on my herpes lesions, I get immediate relief from the itching and burning. Overall cure time has gone from two to four weeks to approximately four days. Taking the neem leaf capsules and tincture simultaneously is definitely responsible for more infrequent occurrences. I gave some cream to a friend and he had the same results." – T.W. - Gainesville, FL

Moles

"I used neem cream on facial moles and they appear to be fading and getting smaller."

Mosquitoes

"On a recent trip to the Amazon rainforest my group used neem insect repellent. We had hours of undisturbed sightseeing and really enjoyed our trip." – M.L. – CA

Pet-Care

"I purchased Neem cream and tincture for the expressed purpose of healing a condition that my dog has with her ears. I have spent hundreds of dollars trying through the veterinarian(s) to clear up the yeast infection and had no suc-

cess until Neem. It worked. I am so happy. So is my dog Breck."
- D.M. - Alexandria, VA

Psoriasis

"I have has psoriasis for about twenty years. Neem cream has been the best product I have used, even better than the prescription medications." - S.A.

"My husband suffered for years with psoriasis on his scalp, face arms and hands. Neem cream has done more for his skin in two weeks than the hundreds of dollars worth of skin products he has tried." - C.D. - Canada

Rash

"I had a persistent rash in the center of my back that was caused by harsh, hot water while bathing. After putting neem lotion on it for only two days it disappeared and never came back."

Scabies

"I had an awful case of scabies on my arms, hands, feet and legs, and progressing to my torso. I went to the doctor and used prescription cream as directed - with no relief at all. I then tried neem soap in the shower in the morning and at night, following the shower with neem lotion applied to my whole body. I felt some relief after the first application, and, after three days, the scabies were gone." - M.B. - Santa Anna, CA

Skin

"The areas I have used neem lotion on have become very soft and have a new feel to it." - E.S. - Leesburg, FL

Sunburn

"My whole family uses neem lotion after going to the beach and we never peel even after getting sunburned. It seems to completely rejuvenate the skin."

Teeth

"Actually I have been using the neem leaf extract 3 drops on the tooth brush... It is green in color but my mouth heals faster than the dentist can believe. I also take two Neem pills every day." – B.B. - Seminole, FL

"After brushing my teeth, I put two droppers of neem leaf extract in a little water or directly in my mouth and swish it around before swallowing. The result is that my gums don't bleed anymore when flossing."

"From the first time I used this (neem) mouthwash mixture, my mouth has never felt more refreshed and clean." – L.L

"After a long trip to India my dentist was surprised that my teeth were in good condition after not seeing him for a year and a half. I give credit to neem, which I included in my tea occasionally."

Urinary

"I recently had a urinary tract infection. I took neem leaf extract for two days and the symptoms were immediately resolved." – E.B. – Colorado

Wart

"I had a wart on my arm for years before I started applying your neem lotion. It's all gone now."

Cautionary Statement

Neem is generally considered an extremely safe product. After centuries of daily ingestion in India where it is used as a toothbrush and placed with food to protect against insects, no danger has been documented. Children in India and Africa eat neem fruit with great enjoyment during its fruiting season. Rats treated with neem oil in laboratory studies actually gained weight instead of showing ill effects. A German study using oil from clean neem seeds showed no toxicity at doses in excess of 5,000 mg per kg (National Research Council, 1992). Tests undertaken for the US Environmental Protection Agency before the approval of a commercial neem product, Margosan-O, showed no or limited toxicity to rats, ducks, rabbits and bees.

However, while consuming large amounts of neem is traditional in Asian and African cultures, caution is still recommended until further research is complete. Its safe use for thousands of years throughout south Asia may be a result of following the prescribed dosages prescribed by the medical practitioners they visited.

❧ VI ❧

Non-Medicinal Uses of Neem

Neem extracts are proving to be some of the best natural, non-toxic methods of controlling insects on food and ornamental crops. Historically, neem has been used for thousands of years to protect food crops and homes from insect pests. Neem leaves are added to rice and sugarcane fields to increase production and reduce pest populations. The natural protection from fungi, bacteria and viruses that neem provides plants is astounding plant scientists everywhere. Neem also has the ability to protect animals and people from insects. Insect repellents made with neem are being used in many tropical countries and have made their way to the United States recently.

Insect Repellent

Summer is the time when most people want to get out and enjoy the outdoors. But biting insects can quickly turn a fun time into a nightmare. Keeping insects away usually involves synthetic repellents containing a potentially dangerous chemical called N, N-diethyl-m-toluamide, commonly called DEET.

Though these repellents are effective they may also be responsible for severe medical problems reported by some people who use them. A safer alternative is needed.

Neem has been used since antiquity as an insect repellent for both people and food crops. One compound (salannin) found in neem leaves, seeds and seed oil is a safer and more effective insect repellent than the widely used chemical ingredient called DEET (N, N-diethyl-m-toluamide) currently found in most commercial repellents (National Research Council, 1992).

Neem extracts tested by the Malaria Institute were found to repel the mosquito that causes malaria for up to twelve hours. Neem provides protection from not only mosquitoes but also from biting flies, sand fleas and ticks. Because of neem's proven effectiveness, insect repellents made with neem are being used in malaria-prone tropical countries.

For those seeking a safe alternative to potentially dangerous synthetic repellents neem offers an attractive alternative for the following reasons:

- Neem oil is an excellent skin moisturizer while DEET is not recommended for repeated application to the skin, around the face or on the hands of small children.

- Neem oil is a natural vegetable oil while DEET is not recommended to be sprayed on furniture, plastics, watch crystals, leather and painted surfaces including automobiles. DEET may actually dissolve all synthetic fabrics but nylon.

- Neem oil has been used safely for centuries while DEET is a synthetic chemical that has only been used for a short time and may pose future unknown health risks. Many researchers believe DEET to be partly responsible for the devastating effects of Gulf War Syndrome.

- Neem is a healing herb that is famous for its wound healing properties. Cuts, scrapes and poison oak and ivy can be salved with neem oil lotions. DEET products contain warnings against getting them in open sores or on damaged skin.

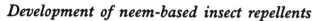

Development of neem-based insect repellents

The tropical region of India is notorious for its mosquitoes and for the number of cases of malaria and other mosquito borne diseases. When the repellent and other anti-insect activity of neem was initially recognized scientists at the Malaria Research Institute began a serious investigation of how best to use neem to protect people from mosquitoes. They began by trying to control mosquitoes where they breed. The researchers placed a small amount of raw neem cake into water where mosquitoes were breeding and waited to see what happened. They discovered that this simple procedure drastically reduced the number of larvae that developed into mosquitoes. Further experiments with more refined neem extracts proved that exposure to neem severely inhibited the ability of mosquito larvae to molt into adult mosquitoes. This was accomplished without the toxic effects on the environment (Boschitz and Grunewald, 1994), (Nagpal *et al*, 1995), (Dhar *et al*, 1996) that result from using the synthetic pesticides typically used to control mosquitoes.

Their next experiments sought to determine how effective neem could be in controlling mosquitoes in the many flooded rice fields of India and Southeast Asia. Rice fields are perfect mosquito breeding grounds; there is a large amount of still water, the fields are usually close to villages where people and livestock provide blood meals, and, because of the expense, the fields are not usually sprayed with insecticides. The researchers selected an economical and eventually very effective way of spreading neem throughout the rice field. The fertilizer that was broadcast on the rice was simply coated with neem extract. The results of the experiment surprised everyone involved. The mosquitoes were almost eliminated and, most surprising, the crop yield of the test field was increased significantly as well. Apparently, the neem-coated fertilizer was able to provide nutrients for a longer period than non-coated fertilizer. (Rao *et al*, 1995) Because of these and many similar experiments with like results, neem coated fertilizers are being used throughout India and Southeast Asia in rice and sugarcane fields. Neem has improved the lives of the people who work in the fields and those who depend upon the crops grown there. The fields are practically free of mosquitoes and the amount of food produced per acre is greater with little additional cost.

Personal Protection

Mosquitoes

Reducing the number of mosquitoes can only accomplish so much. People still must protect their homes and themselves from those that survive. In a series of experiments, scientists have proven that neem is effective at keeping mosquitoes out of the homes of villagers who rarely have windows or screens. When neem oil is mixed with the kerosene used in the lamps of villagers mosquitoes are repelled from the home with only a 1% concentration. Cardboard mats covered with neem oil and placed over a small heater worked equally as well, reducing the number of biting mosquitoes by as much as 83% (Sharma *et al*, 1993b). Even burning neem wood and leaves in cooking fires can keep mosquitoes out of the home or away from campsites (Palsson and Jaenson, 1999). All of these methods are inexpensive and easily practiced by villagers, many of whom have neem trees growing by their homes.

The next experiments narrowed the focus of protection from disease carrying mosquitoes to an individual level. The researchers wanted to find out if neem could be used as an insect repellent for people when applied to the skin. To test this theory volunteers spent all night in the open with skin exposed to entice mosquitoes to bite. Half of the volunteers were covered with a mixture of coconut oil and a 2% concentration of neem oil. The other half were covered in coconut oil alone to act as control for the experiment. Other volunteers, protected by netting, stayed up with a vacuum gun collecting the mosquitoes that landed on each of the volunteers so the number collected could be counted in the morning. The results surpassed all of their expectations. Those who were covered with the coconut oil and neem lotion were completely free of mosquito bites while the control group was subject to several hundred bites. Later experiments showed that a neem oil lotion also protected against the bite of the sand fly, a vector of several serious diseases, oriental sore and the Phlebotomus fever virus (Sharma, 1993c).

The experiments have been carried out primarily to help stop the spread of malaria in tropical regions of the world. But deadly mosquito-borne diseases are no longer rare in North America. We have recently seen the West Nile virus become a problem in the northeast, killing several people. Previously, there were reported over 600 cases of malaria being contracted in Canada in 1995. These cases resulted from travelers with malaria coming into Canada and from mosquito bites from the Anopheles mosquito, a new arrival from the tropics that has now been found in Canada.

Neem is a proven natural and safe repellent against disease-carrying mosquitoes and it has also been reported by users to protect them from other biting insects. I have heard anecdotally that neem oil has repelled the aggressive blackfly and sand fleas as well as it repels mosquitoes.

Ticks

Ticks can spread many types of infections to humans and animals. In North America there are diseases such as Lyme disease, Rocky Mountain spotted fever, Q fever, tularemia, human granulocytic ehrlichiosis, human monocytic ehrlichiosis and several types of viral encephalitis. There are also some ticks that can, through their saliva, cause paralysis of the respiratory tract that can result in death for children and the elderly. Most of the contact with ticks carrying these diseases will be during outdoor activities where you will be able to protect yourself with proper clothing and repellents such as neem.

But, even the common dog tick can be a transmitter of some of these diseases and can be brought right into your home. The American dog tick is the most important vector of the Rocky Mountain spotted fever rickettsia in the eastern U.S. It is also able to transmit the bacteria that causes tularemia (hunter's disease) and has also been found responsible for tick paralysis.

In tests of neem's effectiveness against ticks it was shown to kill 100% of tick larvae after 48 hours (Ndumu *et al*, 1999). When our pets or we go outdoors insects and other biting pests will usually be a part of the experience. Keeping them from biting and possibly transmitting diseases can be accomplished safely with products containing neem oil. The compounds developed over millions of years by the neem tree offer natural, safe and effective protection from insects and other biting pests.

Pets

Pets have various pests that can also afflict people; fleas and ticks are the two most common. As you have already read, ticks can be controlled with neem. Fleas, though usually not associated with many diseases transmitted to humans, (though victims of bubonic plague have an argument about how bad fleas are regarding transmitting disease) can and do cause many problems for both. Many people and pets are allergic to flea bites. They are also extremely annoying.

Keeping these pests from landing or staying on pets, especially when they are taken outside, is something neem can do safely. There are a number of products available that can kill fleas and ticks once they begin feeding on your pet's blood, but it is better to keep them off first. They will therefore not have a chance to bite or to transfer to your carpet or you once your pet returns indoors.

In tests using neem, citronella and DEET as well as combinations of these three insect repellents, neem was by far the most effective repellent. "DEET, with or without neem extract or citronella, and citronella, with or without neem, did not reduce fleas significantly." Neem along with combinations of neem with citronella and DEET were tested on both dogs and cats for the effect against fleas. In the first test for flea repellence on dogs, neem with 1000-2400 ppm azadirachtin reduced fleas 53%-93% for 19 days. However, when neem extract was combined with 500 ppm DEET and 33% w/v citronella, only 500 ppm azadirachtin was needed to reduce fleas 62%-95% for 20 days. When the repellents were tested on cats that had 50 fleas 2 days before treatment, the combination reduced fleas and eggs 100% for almost one week and keep the fleas away (51%-83%) for almost 10 days. The combination killed most fleas within one day and provided effective flea control for 7 days.

Neem alone is a safe and effective repellent. When combined with citronella and trace amounts of DEET neem provides excellent protection for pets. The extremely small (500 ppm) addition of DEET to the formula should pose no health problems since most commercial DEET sprays are from 100,000 ppm (10%) to 500,000 ppm (50%) (Guerrini and Kriticos, 1998).

Neem in Agriculture

As scientists scour rainforests in dangerous and inaccessible areas of the world in search of useful plants, the neem tree grows inconspicuously in the front yards of homes and on college campuses throughout south Asia and Africa. It is this familiarity that had hidden the true miracle of neem until a few scientists took a closer look at this ancient and sacred tree. Researchers worldwide are now focusing on the neem tree and the hundreds of active compounds it produces to try to determine how one tree can do so many things so well.

Agricultural insect control

It is in agriculture that we find most of the research on neem being conducted today. After studying over 250 plants that exhibited insecticidal properties, the consensus of world scientists was that neem proved to be the most effective and most environmentally friendly of them all. Pesticidal products made from neem are just now reaching the attention of the public and can be purchased at agricultural supply houses or ordered through the mail from well-known garden supply manufacturers. Neem promises to provide a truly natural alternative to synthetic insecticides.

In 1990, over 30 million pounds of synthetic insecticides were applied to residential gardens and lawns in the United States. Usually, these insecticides were quick acting nerve toxins designed to kill any insect, including beneficial insects like bees, on contact. Although they are targeted at insects, these broad-spectrum insecticides can harm any creature that lives in or passes through areas where they have been sprayed. This includes earthworms, birds, squirrels, dogs, cats and even people. Most manufacturers of insecticides used in the yard recommend waiting three days before walking barefoot on the sprayed areas and to keep pets and children away for at least that long. As a safety precaution in many cities, signs must be posted to warn the public that a hazardous chemical has been applied to the lawn.

People living as much as a quarter mile away from the insecticide application can be affected by evaporated insecticide and aerosols drifting in the air. In some individuals, this can result in severe reactions like headaches and numbness in the limbs. In others, it can cause less noticeable effects that might never be connected with the true cause of the reaction: toxic insecticides being applied somewhere in the neighborhood.

Applying insecticides is the easiest and most dangerous way to come in contact with them. In south Florida, a man spraying a common yard insecticide went into convulsions and eventually a coma when a wind gust forced the spray back into his face. The nightly news showed a toxic cleanup crew hosing down the area while paramedics in gas masks attended the man laying in his yard.

Had this been a banned product being used by an overzealous individual, it might have been expected. But this was simply a commercial garden insecticide purchased at a local garden supply store; one that was supposed to be safe for anyone to use.

Neem's natural properties pose no danger of toxic reactions. The seeds and leaves of the neem tree are the source of a new class of "soft" pesticides. The term "soft" pesticide is used because no other word quite fits this remarkable product. The main mode of action is as an anti-feedant. Insect pests usually refuse to eat any plant covered with neem and do so until they starve to death. Other effects are as a repellent and a reducer of an insect's ability to reproduce.

Elimination of the insect pest occurs not by quick poisoning, but by starvation and drastic reductions in offspring. Birds and beneficial insects, which are not affected by neem, then feed on the remaining weakened pests and the small number of remaining offspring. The result is an almost-immediate halt to plant damage – without poisoning the environment.

Neem is non-toxic to animals or people. Areas sprayed with neem are not poisonous areas to be avoided for days as are those sprayed with the typical synthetic insecticides. Neem is also a natural, biodegradable product. Only insects that eat plants are affected by neem, leaving honeybees and other beneficial insects essentially unharmed. In fact, in those areas sprayed with neem, the average size and number of earthworms is greater than in unsprayed areas.

The most active insecticidal compound found in neem is azadirachtin, which acts as an anti-feedant. Azadirachtin causes insects to refuse to eat plants sprayed with neem. Insects will land and crawl on the plants but will refuse to eat as long as the azadirachtin is on the plant. In early tests of neem extracts, the desert locust, which is known for its voracious appetite, refused to eat any plants sprayed with neem and eventually starved to death surrounded by its favorite food.

As important as azadirachtin is, neem's true effectiveness comes from the interaction of all the compounds that affect different aspects of an insect's life. Other compounds act as insect repellents, cause insects to lay sterile egg cases, prevent molting, and others simply enhance the effects of other compounds. The number and complexity of the compounds found in neem that affect insects make resistance to neem highly unlikely if properly used. This is extremely important as insects are rapidly developing resistance to the major synthetic insecticides. More and more insects are even developing resistance to natural bacterial controls like *Bacillus thuringensis* (Bt).

In the United States, a stable concentrate of azadirachtin was perfected by Robert Larson in 1985 after more than a decade of work. A more concentrated product is now being marketed to commercial growers. These products have at least a one-year shelf life if stored properly. Because the product is so new and the supply limited, the commercial preparations are relatively expensive, about $30.00 per pint. However, the higher price of the neem product should be weighed against the reduced harm to the environment that it represents. Synthetic pesticides are less expensive in the short run, but factoring in their total impact dramatically increases their true long-term cost.

As a side note, neem has been found to be beneficial to bees. Bees are coming under assault on several fronts. There are mites and diseases that cause bees to produce less pollen and honey and to become sick and die. Neem treated bees showed reduced levels of Nosema and chalkbrood over bees treated with the most current medicines and miticides. Though it appears that azadirachtin is the most active component of the neem compounds, crude neem oil topically applied to the bees provided significant protection against several bee mite species (Melathopoulos *et al*, 2000). The neem treated bees produced three times as much pollen and twice the amount of honey as the non-treated bees (Liu *et al*, 1989).

Agricultural fungicide

Neem provides plants and animals with protection from many types of fungi (Murthy and Sirsi, 1958b), (Bhowmick and Choudharg, 1982), (Schmutterer and Ascher, 1986). In several tests, spraying neem oil on plants prevented the outbreak

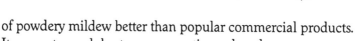

of powdery mildew better than popular commercial products. It seems to work best as a preventive rather than a cure once the fungus has become established.

Neem leaf extracts have also been proven effective against one of the world's most dangerous substances: aflatoxin (Bhatnagar and Zeringue, 1993). Produced by the *Aspergillus flavus* species of mold, aflatoxin is common to grains and nuts (like wheat and peanuts). Only five parts per billion are allowed in food products sold in the U.S. due to its highly carcinogenic nature. Neem leaf extracts sprayed on the grain inhibited the mold from producing the aflatoxins, a finding that could help ensure safer foods and a larger food supply.

Plant viruses

Plant infections caused by plant viruses are difficult to prevent or cure. Recently, however, tests by researchers in India and the United States have shown neem extracts can prevent many types of viral infection and reduce the severity of any damage once there is an outbreak (Saxena *et al*, 1985), (Simons, 1981). The effect is probably a combination of neem's pest control properties and its recognized anti-viral compounds.

Pests flying from an infected plant can carry viruses to uninfected plants, thereby spreading the disease. Reducing the number of disease-carrying insects can therefore help reduce the spread of the virus. Neem also actively inhibits viral diseases. Just as it does with viruses that attack humans and animals, neem prevents the virus from being able to survive outside an infected cell and may also strengthen a plant's ability to fight the infection.

Crops can be protected from viral diseases and their vectors in two ways. First, the field the crops are to be planted in is covered with neem cake and then plowed to work it into the soil. This provides crops long-term and systemic protection for seedlings. Second, the plants are sprayed with neem extracts whenever problems begin to appear. This directly attacks any disease organisms or vectors (insects) and allows the leaves to quickly absorb the effective compounds.

Livestock

Farm animals can also benefit from neem for its protection from insects and disease as well as providing a supplemental food source. In the developing world neem could save untold amounts of money currently spent by farmers on chemical insecticides for their animals. A simple light coating of neem oil keeps biting flies, mosquitoes and ticks away from livestock.

Biting and bothersome insects cause livestock considerable stress and the animals use a lot of energy to try to keep these pests away. Their feeding is often interrupted as they try to dislodge insects from every part of their body. Neem can help eliminate these pests. When a formulation of concentrated neem seed extract was included in the diets of cows the horn fly was practically eliminated (Miller and Chamberlain, 1989). By including the neem extract in the feed insect control could be accomplished wherever the animals receive feed.

Neem Helping Farmers in Developing Countries

Neem's "soft" pesticide is improving the lives of impoverished farmers throughout the tropical range of the neem tree. Substituting crude neem extracts for expensive chemical controls saves both money and lives. In developing countries, an estimated 500,000 people are poisoned and up to 20,000 die annually from using agricultural chemicals. To protect their crops, most of the earnings of farmers in developing countries are spent on these chemicals, producing a cycle that leads not to more food and a better life, but to continued poverty, ill health and environmental degradation.

To break this cycle and to improve the farmer's lives, agencies such as CARE, AID and AFGRO are actively promoting the introduction and use of neem in Southeast Asia, Africa, the Caribbean and both South and Central America. Seedlings and educational programs give the farmers the means and methods for easily making an inexpensive, safe and effective product that protects their crops from over 200 different insect pests, including the desert locust.

Farmers in Mexico and Haiti and shepherds in Australia have begun switching to simple neem-based sprays from the usual synthetic chemical pest controls. This has allowed the farmers to export mangos and other fruit to the United States without the chemical residues that often stopped

NEEM AS SHADE TREE IN AFRICA

their shipments at inspection stations. Neem-based sprays have similarly allowed the shepherds in Australia to produce a pesticide-free wool that is being sold to European buyers for a considerable premium over the standard wool impregnated with chemical pesticides.

Food Storage

Throughout the tropics, much of the food harvested is lost during storage, perhaps as much as 50%. More affluent farmers can and do spray their stored food crops with chemical pesticides to prevent worms, beetles and other infestations. Neem allows impoverished and affluent farmers alike to replace pesticides with a natural and inexpensive alternative. A light coating of neem oil protects stored food crops for up to twenty months from all types of infestations with no deterioration or loss of palatability (Dunkel *et al*, 1995).

Soil amendment - neem cake

After the oil has been pressed from the seed kernels, the remaining material is called "neem cake." This material has been used for many centuries throughout India as a soil amendment. Experience has taught farmers there that working the leftover neem cake into the soil of a garden produces larger, healthier plants that have few problems with insect pests.

CRUSHING NEEM SEEDS

Several studies were done to find out why plants grew better in soils mixed with neem cake. The studies discovered that neem cake was richer in plant nutrients than manure, killed damaging nematodes, promoted larger populations of earthworms, helped keep nitrogen in the soil available for the plants, and provided significant protection from insects. This combination of effects provides an almost ideal growing condition for the plants (Khan *et al*, 1974), (Vijayalakshmi *et al*, 1985).

By killing nematodes in the soil, a major plant pest is eliminated. Nematodes suck the juices from the roots of plants to the point where they are unable to supply sufficient nutrients to the plant. The plants look sickly, fail to grow and may eventually die despite sufficient food, water and care. On the other hand, by promoting larger populations of earthworms, neem cake helps keep the soil loose so that the roots can more easily absorb water and nutrients. Earthworms also enrich the soil by creating readily absorbable nutrients as it feeds on decaying plant material. Neem cake also reduces the nitrification rate of the soil by suppressing nitrifying bacteria such as nitrosomonas and nitrobacter bacteria. This reduces the need for applications of external nutrients. Some studies have shown that mixing neem cake with regularly scheduled applications of manure can almost double crop yield over manure alone. Neem compounds are also slowly absorbed into the plant to augment plant natural defenses with the proven nutritive, antifungal and insect repellent properties of neem.

**THREE YEAR-OLD
NEEM TREE FROM SEED**

❧ VII ❧

Botanical Description and Cultivation

The neem tree (*Azadirachta indica*) is a tropical evergreen related to mahogany. Native to east India and Burma, it grows in much of Southeast Asia and west Africa. A few trees have recently been planted in the Caribbean and several Central American countries. Outdoors, in locations where temperatures don't drop much below freezing, it may reach up to 50 feet tall. It will grow where rainfall is as little as 18 inches per year and thrives in areas that experience extreme heat of up to 120° F. They are reported to live for up to 200 years.

Its blooms are small, white flowers with a very sweet, jasmine-like scent. Its edible fruit – loved by children in Africa – is about 3/4 of an inch long. A neem tree generally begins bearing fruit at three to five years old, and can produce up to 110 lbs. of fruit annually when mature.

Since neem is a tropical tree, it must be protected from hard freezes. In northern climates it may be grown in pots with the care and appearance of the more-common fichus tree.

Neem makes an ideal indoor plant because it grows well with a minimum of maintenance. For optimum growth, neem should be placed near a sunny window during the winter and moved outside during summer months. However, they will survive indoors even if they don't receive any natural light at all. They also should be grown in a pot as large as possible or their growth will be stunted to remain proportionate in size with their root system.

Whether grown indoors or out, neem trees must have well-drained soil. They are relatively heavy feeders, responding to organic fertilizers such as fish emulsion, bone meal and kelp with lush new growth. If leaves begin to turn yellow, the tree has been given too much fertilizer or water. Although neem trees are evergreen, they often lose their leaves in very dry periods or after a hard frost. Neem trees will quickly revive with regular watering or the onset of warm summer days.

NEEM FLOWERS

Few pests attack the neem tree and most problems with neem are directly related to over-watering. Several different types of fungal diseases can cause dieback, and slugs that thrive in soggy spaces will eat the bottom leaves of small trees.

Other Species of Neem and plants confused with neem

There are two other known distinct species of neem. These are

Azadirachta siamensis (Syn. *A. azadirachta* var. *siamensis*) and *Azadirachta excelsa*. There are also different ecotypes of each species and crosses between species. For the most part the compounds found in each species of neem tree are the same, though the relative percentages of each compound may vary. However, there are compounds found in each that are unique to the individual species. Further research will probably better define these differences.

Azadirachta siamensis

In Thailand, the seeds and young leaves of this species, called "sweet" neem, are used as additions to many foods as spices. The *A. siamensis* compounds are similar to those of the Indian neem but the leaves, which are about twice as large as *A. indica*, are less bitter. The seeds are also considerably larger and the kernels are an emerald green rather than white. The characteristic garlic-like smell is still there and so is the very bitter taste. However, *A. siamensis* has a spicy, hot tinge that supplements the taste of the seed.

The medicinal uses of *A. siamensis* in Thailand are similar to those of *A. indica* in India. Merchants and emigrants carried much of the Indian tradition of medicine to Thailand and the rest of southeast Asia over the thousands of years that these ancient cultures have been trading with each other. Neem did not attain the religious significance that it did in India and was not a pervasive influence on the daily life of the Thai people. However, it was recognized for the qualities of healing and good health that neem is known for everywhere (Dr. David Lee, personal communication).

Azadirachta excelsa

There is one other recognized species of neem that grows in remote areas of Malaysia and the Philippine islands called *Azadirachta excelsa*. This species grows up to 160 feet tall deep in the mostly inaccessible rainforests. The tree is protected by the government from logging and the distribution of the seeds is strictly controlled. Due to its rarity and location in remote areas, only scientific or conservation use is permitted and few seeds are allowed out of the country. Because of its scarcity this species of neem, like *A. siamensis*, is not used extensively for commercial products. It is used in some indigenous medicines for such problems as stomach ulcers, skin problems, malaria and as a general tonic against illness. As in Thailand, some of the Indian medical tradition was transferred to these areas by travelers over the centuries. Neem became a part of the combined medical culture of the peoples of these countries.

Though the three species of neem trees differ in appearance, the usefulness of the medicinal compounds in each species was recognized and used by healers throughout southeast Asia. Limonoids from A. excelsa exhibited the same anti-cancer activity as A. indica providing more evidence of the medicinal value of this species (Cui *et al*, 1998). As researchers in these countries begin understanding the true possibilities of these trees, greater emphasis is being placed on protecting the available varieties. They are also promoting the establishment of plantations of neem trees to be able to supply the growing demand for the commercial products that can be obtained from them (Dr. David Lee, personal communication).

Chinaberry is Not Neem

For many years there was, and apparently continues to be, some confusion regarding the common chinaberry tree and neem. The scientific name for the chinaberry tree is *Melia Azedarach* and commonly called Persian lilac while neem's scientific name was *Melia azadirachta* and the common name was Indian lilac. This was an easy thing to get confused about. Now neem has the scientific name of *Azadirachta indica* but considerable old information is available that sometimes confuses the two.

The possibility for confusion is obvious. The fact that they look very similar on first glance also added to the confusion. Though they share similar traits, chinaberry has one major drawback; it is toxic. Unless the person using chinaberry is very knowledgeable and skilled in its use chinaberry can cause severe health problems and even death.

Chinaberry is a regular sight in the southern United States. Here in Florida it is even considered a pest plant because it grows readily almost everywhere. During the late summer they can easily be located by the hundreds of drupes of bright yellow seeds hanging from almost every branch with few leaves to hide them. When I was first introducing neem to gardeners and natural health practitioners they told me they had trees growing in their yards just like the ones I was promoting. I had to strongly warn them to leave their tree alone and not try to use it for the same things for which neem can be used. Eating a few leaves can make you very sick and eating chinaberry fruit can put you in the hospital under intensive care.

The easiest way to be sure you are using true neem is to purchase the products from a reputable supplier. If you are going to grow your own neem tree be sure the person selling the tree is well known and has experience in telling the difference. The differences are subtle but easy to find if you know what to look for.

The first thing to look for is the leaf:

1) Neem leaves are somewhat glossy and have a fine texture while chinaberry leaves are very glossy and very smooth.

2) New leaves on neem trees are frequently red while chinaberry is always green.

3) By breaking open the leaves the difference is also telling. When neem leaves are crushed between the fingers to release the oils inside they smell of a light spice while chinaberry smells like mown grass.

4) To get the real difference you have to crush the leaves and put a very small amount in your mouth (even if it is chinaberry this amount will not hurt you). Neem tastes very bitter and stays on the tongue while chinaberry has almost no taste whatever.

The next thing to look for is the fruit and the seed inside:

1) Neem fruit will turn yellow and be very soft with the seeds

coming out with the slightest squeeze while chinaberry fruit stays hard and the seed has to be cut from the fruit.

2) Neem seeds have a jelly-like coating that has a somewhat sweet taste while chinaberry has none.

3) Neem seeds are smooth and teardrop shaped while chinaberry has grooves running the length of the oval seed.

CHINABERRY SEED (LEFT)
NEEM SEED (RIGHT)

The last thing to look for is the flower:

1) Neem flowers are white petals and a yellow center while chinaberry is white petals with a purple center. Both flowers have a light scent with a hint of jasmine.

Medicinal Properties of Chinaberry

Chinaberry has been investigated for medicinal properties because Ayurvedic practitioners have used it in some of their preparations. Neem and chinaberry have similar anti-viral and cytotoxic liminoid compounds, which is not surprising since they both belong to the Melia family. Several Azadirachtin-like compounds were purified from ethanol extracts of chinaberry root bark, which were toxic to lymphocytic leukemia (Itokawa *et al*, 1995). A compound called Meliacine inhibited the replication of foot and mouth disease virus and polio virus (Wachsman and Coto, 1995) and blocked the virus from penetrating cell walls and from releasing infectious particles into the cellular medium (Castilla *et al*, 1998). Another compound inhibited the replication of herpes simplex virus-1 (Kim *et al*, 1999).

The leaves of the chinaberry contain a number of antiviral compounds. In all of the experiments the leaves were subjected to a wide array of purification techniques to come up with a compound that exhibited anti-viral properties without also being toxic. In early tests leaf compounds had broad-spectrum anti-viral activity (Andrei *et al*, 1985). The leaf compounds were extremely effective at reducing virus yield after infection by 99% without being toxic (Descalzo and Coto, 1989). The extracts act directly on the ability of the virus to replicate and infect cells, not by inducing an interferon production increase (Andrei *et al*, 1988).

The fruit of the chinaberry also contain some medicinal compounds. When specific extracts of the fruit were given to rats that had induced ulcers the rats showed decreases in the acidity of the gastric juices and reduced the ulcers by over 80 percent in 10 days of treatment. (Hanifa and Al-Khatib, 1984). These compounds required purification and isolation to be safe and effective, therefore no chinaberry fruit should ever be eaten or in any way ingested.

Though chinaberry and neem are from the same family, chinaberry should never be confused with neem. Neem is a safe and effective herb with thousand of years of testing and usage behind it. Ongoing tests continue to illustrate the lack of toxicity of neem and neem extracts. However, chinaberry is a tree with a long history of causing harm to those who ingest any part of the tree. It is only marginally effective as a plant pest toxin but plants sprayed with chinaberry extracts should be treated the same as you would any toxic pesticide.

Chinaberry trees should be removed from your yard if you have small children or pets that might put chinaberry fruit in their mouth. Children have died from eating 6 to 8 ripe fruits. Two dogs that ate a few chinaberry fruit developed signs of poisoning within a few hours. Though the dogs received emergency treatment, neither dog survived longer than 36 hours (Hare *et al*, 1997). Such poisonings are rare but the potential is there as long as the chinaberry tree is within reach of small children and pets.

"Cooking" Neem

If you go into almost any Indian store that carries food items and ask for "neem" they will usually assume you are asking for curry leaf also known as "cooking" neem. They will usually have a small bag of fresh leaves but sometimes some small plants so you can have fresh curry leaf at any time. Curry leaf is considered a relative of neem and is used extensively in Keralite cuisine as a seasoning and flavor enhancer similar in use to bay leaves.

Curry leaf has a few verified medicinal properties but its main use is as a spice. Investigation of curry leaf shows that it has beneficial effects on the liver, heart and kidneys (Khan *et al*, 1996a). Rats fed on 10% curry leaf had reduced total serum cholesterol levels, LDL and VLDL and an increase in HDL showing that it is beneficial for cholesterol management (Khan *et al*, 1996b). Curry leaf even has anti-oxidant properties (Khan *et al*, 1997) while also providing hypoglycemic activity (Khan *et al*, 1995). The root bark, which is not an edible portion of the plant, showed weak cytotoxicity against melanoma and leukemia cell lines (Chakrabarty *et al*, 1997).

Though not a "neem", curry leaf is invaluable as a cooking spice for many south Asian cuisines. It would be a nice addition to any garden, especially for those who enjoy cooking. That there are also health benefits for those who use "cooking" neem in their food preparations is a wonderful bonus for this great tasting spice.

Growing Neem for Home Use

Neem seedlings and indoor plants can be obtained from several growers in Florida and California. The seeds of the neem tree can also be purchased but they are available only for a short time in late summer. They are viable for only a few weeks so they must be planted immediately. Neem will have to be grown as an indoor plant in areas where hard freezes occur. Outdoors, neem trees have to be protected from frosts until two years old, even in warmer areas. The tree will only get as large as the container will allow, so a minimum ten-gallon container is recommended.

Neem trees that are pruned often for their leaves and twigs will become short and bushy. If pruned in early spring, the number of flowers and fruit produced may be reduced. There-fore, it is recommended that pruning branches or picking large numbers of leaves should be postponed until after the fruit has ripened. Any extra leaves picked during the remainder of the growing season can be dried and stored for use during the winter and early spring.

Neem grown at home for personal medicinal use should be organically cultivated, picked fresh and stored as carefully as possible. The leaves can be dried and stored in a powdered form and used as a tea or extracts made by macerating (soak) in alcohol for a month.

POTTED INDOOR NEEM TREE

To obtain the rich neem oil, the fruit should be picked when it becomes a nice yellow color. The seed can be simply squeezed from the fruit leaving a clear jell on the seed. This jell must be re-moved for proper seed preparation. The jell comes off easily by putting the jell-coated seeds in a container of water, grabbing a handful of seeds and rubbing them between your hands a few times until all of the seeds are free of the jell. The clean neem seeds are then dried for a couple of days in the shade. Next, remove the seed husk by crushing the seeds with a rolling pin between two layers of cloth and picking out the kernels. Finally, put the kernels into a closed container in the refrigerator and throw the husks into the garden. To get the oil from the kernels they can either be pressed with a hydraulic press or macerated with sesame oil for two weeks. The neem oil can then be added to a lotion and used as directed in the earlier chapters.

Growing neem from seeds

Place the seeds in a shallow dish with enough warm water to cover the seeds. Leave for 24 hours. Remove the seeds and place them on a wet paper towel and cover with another wet paper towel and place in a window with full sun. Keep the paper wet. Check the seeds daily to see if the seeds germinate. Within 3 to 4 days the seeds should have a root tail coming from one end of the seed. As soon as the seed tail appears place the seed in a container with moist, but not wet, potting soil and place the container in a window with direct sun. Do not place the pot where the heat builds up and dries out the soil quickly. If necessary, place a small shade screen in front of the pot so the seedling receives diffused sunlight. Lightly fertilize once with tropical indoor fertilizer. Neem will die if the soil is soaked, therefore test the bottom of the container to be sure it is moist but not soaked. When the seedling reaches 3 inches, transfer the plant to a container of at least a gallon in size. Keep the plant in the sun. When the threat of frost is over place the plant outdoors under a light shade cloth. Fertilize lightly every other week with a citrus or other full spectrum fertilizer.

DANGER! If the tree has had too little sun during the winter and it is placed in the direct sun, the leaves will turn white and the tree will die!

When the plant reaches one foot in height place the plant in a container of at least 5 gallons in size. Continue fertilizing every other week. The plant should be between three and five feet tall after one year. If you want an indoor plant, cut the plant to two feet and it will branch out and become bushier. Keep bumping the plant into larger pots as needed and prune as necessary to maintain the height suitable for you home. If it is to be outdoors where there are no freezes, watch it grow as it quickly becomes a twenty to thirty foot shade tree in five years.

Home Preparation
of Neem Products

Many people who own their own neem trees want to make products out of the leaves, oil and bark of the tree. They are fairly simple to make with just a little time and effort. Dr. Puri has provided some recipes for those who want to try their hand at something that can be very enjoyable and rewarding.

Neem Shampoo

Ingredients:		
	coconut oil	3 oz
	neem oil	1 oz
	caustic soda	2 oz
	orange oil	1/4 tsp
	camphor oil	1/4 tsp
	water	6 oz
	fragrance	8 drops

Combine the neem oil, camphor oil and the orange oil. Heat this mixture of oils to 100° F. Add the caustic soda to the water and stir until all of the soda is dissolved. Add the water-soda mixture slowly to the heated coconut oil and stir for 15 minutes. Add fragrance and stir for 1 minute. Let cool and place into bottles for use.

Neem Soap

Ingredients:		
	neem oil	28 oz
	coconut oil	8 oz
	caustic soda	3 oz
	fragrance	1 tsp
	water	32 oz

Combine the neem and camphor oil and heat this mixture of oils to 100° F. Add the caustic soda to the water and stir until all of the soda is dissolved. Add the water-soda mixture slowly to the heated coconut oil and stir for 15 minutes or until the mixture is the consistency of batter. Add the fragrance and stir for 1 minute. Pour the mixture into a cake pan lightly coated with cornstarch. When the soap is just hard enough, cut the soap into bars. When the soap is hard enough to resist pressure from your finger remove the bars from the pan and set out for three weeks to fully harden.

First Aid Balm

Ingredients:	neem oil	28 oz
	bees wax	8 oz
	eucalyptus oil	1/2 tsp
	wintergreen oil	1 tsp
	mint oil	1 oz

Heat the bees wax and neem oil together until they melt and mix. Let cool until the mixture is 100º F then add the other oils and stir for one minute.

*This is not for cuts or abrasions but for aches, pains and inflammation. For congestion place one teaspoon in a cup of very hot water and inhale the vapors.

Neem Cream

Ingredients:	neem oil	2 oz
	almond oil	8 oz
	bees wax	4 oz
	zinc oxide	1 oz
	boric acid	1/4 tsp
	water	6 oz
	fragrance	4 drops

Dissolve the beeswax into the oil by heating the beeswax, neem oil and almond oil to 100º F, stirring until thoroughly dissolved. In a separate container heat the water to 100º F and dissolve the boric acid into it. Mix the two containers together while still hot and stir until the mixture has cooled to lukewarm. Add the zinc oxide and fragrance and stir until cool.

Neem Baby Oil

Ingredients:	sesame oil	9 oz
	neem oil	1 oz
	sandal oil	1 tsp

Simply mix the oils together while luke warm and stir for one minute. No fragrance is needed because of the natural aroma of the sandal oil.

Neem Baby Powder

Ingredients:	cornstarch	7 oz
	neem leaf powder	1 oz
	neem oil	10 drops

Place the cornstarch and neem leaf powders in a fine flower sifter and add the neem oil to the top of the powders. Run the material through the sifter at least five times until the powder has all been combined with the neem oil and no clumping occurs. Place the powder in a clean container, preferably one with holes such as a large salt shaker.

Neem Face Pack

Ingredients:	neem leaves	2 oz
	orange peel	2 oz
	kaolin (clay)	12 oz
	boric acid	1 oz
	fragrance	1 tsp

The neem leaves and orange peel must be dried and finely ground. The ingredients are then thoroughly mixed in a blender and placed in a container. When ready for use add enough water to make a paste and apply to the face and allow to dry. Wash the face with warm water to remove.

Neem Tooth Powder

Ingredients:	neem bark powder	1 oz
	baking soda	1 oz
	calcium carbonate	2 oz
	fine clove powder	1/4 oz

All of the powders are mixed together and run through a fine flower sifter several times. If you want to make a toothpaste out of this powder add water until you have the desired consistency then add a little vegetable glycerin and mix vigorously for a minute or two. Place into a small jar that can be sealed after each use.

If you have no neem bark powder you may substitute neem leaf powder but the taste will be more bitter. Mixing in a little stevia to taste will help eliminate this condition.

Neem Hemorrhoid Cream

Ingredients:		
	neem bark powder	4 oz
	neem oil	1/4 tsp
	alum powder	1 oz
	vegetable glycerin	8 oz

Add all of the ingredients in a bowl and thoroughly mix until a paste is formed.

Neem Hair Tonic

Ingredients:		
	neem oil	1 tsp
	almond oil	4 oz
	cayenne pepper	1/4 oz
	camphor oil	2 drops
	rubbing alcohol	1/4 tsp

Place the neem oil, almond oil and cayenne pepper in a sealed glass jar and place in a window with direct sunlight for one week. Filter the mixture through a coffee filter to remove the pepper particles. Dissolve the camphor oil in the alcohol and add to the oils, mixing thoroughly.

Place a tablespoon of this tonic into your hand and rub vigorously into the scalp. Cover the hair with a plastic cap for thirty minutes and wash out with a neem shampoo.

Bath Potpourri

Ingredients:		
	neem leaves	1 lb
	neem bark	4 oz
	neem flowers	1/4 oz
	clove powder	1/2 oz
	camphor oil	2 drops

rubbing alcohol 1/4 tsp

Course grind and mix the ingredients in a blender, then place into a sealed container. For each bath place four tablespoons of the material into a cotton bag and leave it under the water faucet while the bath is filling.

Note: If neem flowers are unavailable substitute chamomile or lavender.

Wound Poultice

Ingredients: neem leaf 1 lb

neem bark 4 oz

Course grind and mix the ingredients in a blender then place into a sealed container. When needed take one cup of the mixture and place in a bowl. Add simmering hot water and stir until all the powder is wet. Let cool to the touch. Place the mixture into a nylon bag and secure to the wound with a cotton cloth. Leave on for several hours. Repeat daily as needed. When you have a muscle sprain, bruise or skin wound a neem poultice will relieve the pain, reduce swelling and speed healing. A neem poultice can help heal wounds that do not respond well to other treatments, such as the slow healing wounds of diabetics.

Pet Skin Care

Ingredients: neem oil 1 oz

lemon peel 1 oz

cedar wood 1 oz

vegetable oil 10 oz

camphor oil 2 drops

Place all of the ingredients in a blender and mix to a fine slurry. Place the mixture in a glass container in the sun for one week. Filter out the particles through a fine cloth or nylon mesh and place in a glass jar. After each bath take a small amount and rub vigorously into the skin.

Pet Vitalizer

Ingredients		
	neem leaf	8 oz
	garlic powder	1/2 oz
	brewers yeast	1/2 oz
	soy bacon bits	4 oz

Place all the contents into a blender and grind them into a fine powder. Place into a salt shaker. Add 1/4 gram (a few shakes) for every 10 pounds the pet weighs. This mixture is good for old, infirm or arthritic pets. It has even helped pets recover from diseases and operations.

Insect Repellent

Ingredients:		
	neem oil	1/2 oz
	neem leaf	4 oz
	grain alcohol	2 oz
	water	3 oz
	aloe vera juice	4 oz
	lemongrass oil	1/2 oz
	lemon peel	1 oz
	cedar wood oil	1/4 oz
	coconut oil	1 oz
	dish detergent	1/2 oz

Place the neem leaf, grain alcohol, aloe vera juice and water into a glass container and leave on a shelf for one month, turning over once per day. When complete strain the contents through a coffee filter. Mix the remaining ingredients together and heat to 100° F. Combine the leaf extract with the warmed mixture and stir for five minutes and let cool. Place the contents in a spray or squeeze bottle for ease of application. Shake the contents before each use.

Roach Sterilizer

Ingredients		
	neem leaf	6 oz
	neem oil	6 drops

curry leaf	6 oz
banana	4 oz

Place the ingredients into a blender and mix until it is a fine, wet powder. Place the contents on a plate and let dry for a day. Run the dry material through a sifter to turn it into a powder again. Add a pinch of this powder to a small piece of bread and roll it between your hands until the powder is thoroughly mixed into the bread. Place the bread balls in cupboards or behind appliances. Replace after a few days. The powder will cause roaches to reduce their offspring to as low as zero.

Appendix

❧ I ❦

Glossary

analgesic:	Pain relief.
antigen:	A substance capable of creating an immune response.
anthelminthic:	Kills or prevents the growth of parasites and intestinal worms.
anti-inflammatory:	Reduces inflammation in tissues.
antipyretic:	Fever reducing.
antiseptic:	Kills or prevents the growth of bacteria.
anti-viral:	Kills or prevents the growth of viruses.
arrhythmic:	Irregularity of the heartbeat in either force or timing.
Ayurvedic:	Natural healing system of India.
catechin:	Plant substance with astringent properties.
CD8+ lymphocyte:	A critical subpopulation of cytotoxic and suppressor

T-lymphocytes.

cornucopia: Indicating something in abundance.

corticosteroid: Hormone important in protein and carbohydrate metabolism.

cystitis: Inflammation of the urinary bladder.

decoction: Extraction obtained by boiling.

epidermal: Outer layer of the skin.

extract: A substance obtained with and contained in a solvent.

flavonoid: Antibacterial and antifungal aromatic compound.

histamine: Dilates and increases permeability of blood vessels.

hypertension: Abnormally high blood pressure.

immunomodulatory: Ability to change the immune response.

immunosuppressive: Retard the effects of the natural immune response.

interferon: Agent that acts against viruses and can help combat cancer.

intrauterine: Situated within the uterus.

in vitro: Outside a living body.

in vivo: Inside a living body.

limonoids: A compound that sometimes gives citrus a bitter taste.

meningitis: Inflammation of the membrane around the brain and spinal cord.

peritonitis: Bacterial disease causing inflammation of the stomach's membrane.

phenolic: A type of organic compound.

polysaccharides: A complex carbohydrate.

poultice: Heated medicinal material placed

over sores and held with a bandage.

prostaglandin: Fatty acid that performs hormone-like actions.

protozoa: Single celled animals that are often parasites to humans.

spermatogenesis: Formation of sperm inside the male.

tincture: Medicinal substance in an alcoholic solution.

T-lymphocyte: Lymphoid cells concerned with cell-mediated immunity.

TNF: Tumor Necrosis Factor. A tumor inhibiting factor.

vasodilation: Enlargement of the blood vessels to allow greater blood flow.

❧ II ❧

Neem in the Wamirithu Herbal Clinic, Kenya

In rural Kenya there are few hospitals and limited access to Western medicines. There are, however, fine doctors and medical practitioners who want to help people and who use whatever they have available that can help heal. Kenya and the rest of Africa have a long tradition of using the many medicinal plants of the region. In addition, in the last century Indian immigrants introduced neem trees to the area. The Neem Association sent a draft copy of this book to the Director of the Wamirithu Herbal Clinic in Kenya, Samwel W. Kihia. The hope was that it would give insight to the potential healing powers of neem as shown by the many scientific research papers cited in the book. After one year of using neem for some of the ailments the Wamirithu Herbal Clinic reported the following:

Ulcers - Resolution of 80% of the cases. Drink one glass three times a day of neem leaf extract made by boiling 5g of neem leaves, 15g of brown olives (for taste) in 3 liters of water for 20 min.

Gout - Elimination of the problem within one week. Drink one glass three times a day of neem leaf extract made by boiling 5g of neem leaves in 2 liters of water for 20 min.

Diabetes - Effective at managing the disease and, in some cases, healing after some time. Drink one glass a day of neem leaf extract made by boiling 10g of neem leaves in 2 liters of water for 20 min.

Pneumonia - Completely cured in 3 weeks. Drink one glass a day of hot neem leaf extract made by boiling 2g of neem leaves in one cup of water for 20 min.

Chest related cases - Clears the chest within 3 days. Drink one glass a day of hot neem leaf extract made by boiling 2g of neem leaves in one cup of water for 20 min.

Malaria - Cures the disease completely in one week, very good in persistent cases. Drink one glass three times a day of neem leaf extract made by boiling 30g of neem leaves in 3 liters of water for 20 min.

Appendix

❧ III ❧

Patents on Neem

United States

1) 5,900,493. Triterpine derivatives of Azadirachtin having insect antifeedant and growth inhibitory activity.

2) 5,886,029. Method and composition for treatment of diabetes.

3) 5,885,600. Natural insect repellent formula and making of same.

4) 5,856,526. Pesticidal dry powder formulation enriched in Azadirachtin up to 88%...

5) 5,840,669. Herbal dry cleaning powder composition.

6) 5,827,521. Shelf stable insect repellent, insect growth regulator and insecticidal formulas.

7) 5,824,291. Chewing gum containing a teeth-whitening agent.

8) 5,730,986. Process for the isolation of an active principal from azadirachta indica useful for controlling gastric hyperacidity and gastric ulceration.

9) 5,698,423. Method for producing Azadirachtin by cell culture of Azadirachta indica.

10) 5,695,763. Method for the production of storage stable Azadirachtin from seed kernels of the neem tree.

11) 5,679,662. Synergistic use of Azadirachtin and pyrethrum.

12) 5,626,848. Reduced-cloud-point clarified neem oil and methods of producing.

13) 5,591,436. Composition for a dietary supplement for the treatment of hemorrhoids.

15) 5,472,700. Combinations of neem seed extract and bifenthrin for control of ectoparasite in animals.

3) 5,501,855. Neem oil as a male contraceptive.

3) 5,420,318. Preparation of high purity neem seed extracts.

5) 5,411,736. Hydrophobic extracted neem oil - a novel insecticide.

6) 5,409,708. Fungicidal compositions derived from neem oil and neem wax fractions.

7) 5,397,571. Co-extraction of Azadirachtin and neem oil.

8) 5,395,951. Triterpine derivatives of Azadirachtin having antifeedant and growth inhibitory activity and a process for extracting such compounds from the neem plant.

9) 5,391,779. Stable extracts from neem seeds.

10) 5,372,817. Insecticidal compositions derived from neem oil and neem wax fractions.

11) 5,371,254. Preparation of edible neem oil.

12) 5,370,873. Therapeutic compounds derived from the neem tree.

13) 5,368,856. Hydrophobic extracted neem oil - a novel fungicide.

14) 5,352,697. Storage stable pesticide compositions comprising Azadirachtin and epoxide.

15) 5,352,672. Acaricidal combinations of neem seed extract and bifenthrin.

16) 5,298,251. Fungicide compositions derived from neem oil and neem wax fractions.

16) 5,298,247. Neem oil fatty acid distillation residue based pesticide.

17) 5,281,618. Storage stable high Azadirachtin solution.

18) 5,229,007. Selective removal of aflatoxin from Azadirachtin containing compositions.

18) 5,196,197. Reversible fertility control for prevention of pregnancy in females.

19) 5,124,349. Storage stable Azadirachtin formulation.

20) 5,110,591. Neem oil emulsifier.

21) 5,047,242. Azadirachtin derivative insecticides.

22) 5,009,886. Dentifrice.

23) 4,960,791. Salannin derivative insect control agents.

24) 4,946,681. Method to prepare an improved storage stable neem seed extract.

25) 4,943,434. Insecticidal hydrogenated neem extracts.

26) 4,923,713. Azadirachtin-like compounds and insect-destroying agents containing them.

27) 4,556,562. Stable anti-pest neem seed extract.

28) 4,537,774. Hot-water extracts of neem bark.

29) 4,536,496. Polysaccharides N9GI, Their preparation and therapeutic compositions containing them.

30) 4,515,785. Neem bark extracts.

31) 4,223,003. Paste and powder dentifrices.

14) H1, 541. Method for producing Azadirachtin concentrates from neem seed materials.

Select Foreign Patents on Neem

1) Production of antitumor polysaccharide N9G1 from Melia azadirachta (neem) bark. Jpn. Kokai Tokkyo Koho JP 60, 10717(85 19,717)(c1.A61k35/78), 31 Jan 1985 Chem Abstr., 103(8): 348, abstr.

2) Isolation of anti-inflammatory polysaccharides from Melia azadirachta (neem). Jpn. Kokai Tokkyo Koho JP 58,225, 022), (c1.A61K35/78), 27 Dec. 1983. Chem Abstr., 100(12):351, abstr. 9135n, 1984.

3) Preparation of antitumor polysaccharide (N9G1) from Melia azadirachta (neem). Jpn. Kokai Tokkyo Koho JP 60, 42, 328)(C1.A61K35/78), 6 Mar. 1985. Chem Abstr., 102 (26): 346, abstr. 226032y, 1985.

❧ IV ❧

Bibliography

Abatan, M.O., & Makinde, M.J., (1986). Screening Azadirachta indica and Pisum sativum for possible antimalarial activities. Journal of Ethnopharmacology. 17: 85-93.

Alam, M.M., Siddiqui, M.B., & Husain, W. (1989). Treatment of diabetes through herbal drugs in rural India. Fitoterapia. Vol. LXI, No. 3. 240 - 242.

Almas, K. (1999). The antimicrobial effects of extracts of Azadirachta-indica (Neem) and Salvador persica (Arak) chewing sticks. Indian J Dent Res. Jan-Mar;10(1):23-6.

Anderson, D.M.W., Hendrie, A., & Munro, A.C., (1972). The amino acid and amino sugar composition of some plant gums. Phytochemistry. Vol. 11, pp.733-736.

Andrei, G.M., Coto, C.E., & de Torres, R.A. (1985). Assays of cytotoxicity and antiviral activity of crude and semipurified extracts of green leaves of Melia azedarach L. Rev Argent Microbiol. 17(4):187-94.

Andrei, G.M., Damonte, E.B., de Torres, R.A., & Coto, C.E. (1988). Induction of a refractory state to viral infection in mammalian cells by a plant inhibitor isolated from leaves of the Melia azedarach L. Antiviral Res. Jul;9(4):221-31.

Arivazhagan, S., Balasenthil, S., & Nagini, S. (2000). Modulatory effects of garlic and neem leaf extracts on N-methyl-N'nitro-N'nitrosoguanidine (MNNG)-induced oxidative stress in Wistar rats. Cell-Biochem-Funct. Mar; 18(1) 17-21.

141

Badam, L., Deolankar, R.P., Kulkarrni, M.M., Nagsampgi, B.A. & Wagh, U.V. (1987). 'In vitro' antimalarial activity of neem (Azadirachta indica) leaf and seed extracts. Indian Journal of Malariology. 24: 111-117.

Badam, L., Joshi, S.P., & Bedekar, S.S. (1999). 'In vitro' antiviral activity of neem (Azadirachta indica. A. Juss) leaf extract against group B coxsackieviruses. J Commun Dis. Jun;31(2):79-90.

Bains, S.S., Prasad, R. & Bhatia, P.C. (1971). Use of indigenous materials to enhance the efficiency of fertilizer nitrogen for rice. Fert. News. 16: 30-30, 52.

Balasenthil, S., Arivazhagan, S., Ramachandran, C.R., Ramachandran, V., & Nagini, S. (1999). Chemopreventive potential of neem (Azadirachta indica) on 7,12-dimethylbenz[a]anthracene (DMBA) induced hamster buccal pouch carcinogenesis. J-Ethnopharmacol. Nov.1; 67(2):189-95.

Bannerjee, S., & Rembold, H. (1992). Azadirachtin A interferes with control of serotonin pools in the neuroendocrine system of locusts. Naturwissenschaften. Feb; 79(2): 81-4.

Bannerjee, S. (1994). Serotonin immunoreactivity and its content in Azadirachtin treated locusts. Proceedings of the Academy of Environmental Biology; 3(1): 25-31.

Banerji, R., & Nigam, S.K., (1983). Anti-proteolytic activity of some triterpenoids, J. Crude Drug Res., 21, No.2: 93-5.

Barde, A.K., & Singh, S.M. (1983). Activity of plant extracts against scytalidium anamorph of hendersonula toruloidea causing skin and nail diseases in man. Indian Drugs, 362-4.

Bardhan, J., Riar, S.S., Sawhney, R.C., Kain, A.K., Thomas, P., & Ilavazhagan, G. (1991). Neem oil - a fertility controlling agent in rhesus monkeys. Indian J. Physiol Pharmacol. Oct 35(4): 278-80.

Basak, S.P. & Chakraborty, D.P. (1968). Chemical investigation of azadirachta indica leaf (Melia azadirachta). Journal of the Indian Chemical Society. Vol 45(5): 466-7.

Basu, A. (1956). A specific for leucoderma. Journal, Bombay Nat. Hist. Society. 53(4): 743-45.

Batra, C.P., Mittal, P.K., Adak, T., & Sharma, V.P. (1998). Efficacy of neem oil-water emulsion against mosquito immatures. Indian J Malariol. Mar; 35(1): 15-21.

Bawasakar, V.S., Mane, D.A., Hapse, D.G. & Zende, G.K. (1980). Use of neem (Azadirachta indica) cake as a blending material for economy in sugarcane Coop, Sugar. 11(8): 1-7.

Beard, J. (1989). Tree may hold the key to curbing Chagas' parasite. New Scientist, Oct.: 31.

Beardsley, T. (1992). Cellular response: are antibodies the most effective against AIDS? Scientific American December 1992,: 42-4.

Bhandari, P.R., & Mukerji, B.(1959). The neem: Indian lilac (Azadirachta indica). The Eastern Pharmacist, Jan.;2(13): 21-4.

Bhanwra, S., Singh, J., & Khosla, P. (2000). Effect of Azadirachta indica (Neem) leaf aqueous extract on paracetamol-induced liver damage in rats. Indian J Physiol Pharmacol. Jan;44(1):64-8.

Bhargava, A.K. (1987). Neem oil as a synergist to anti-diabetic drugs for management of secondary hyperglycemia. Neem Newsletter, 4(3): 31-2.

Bhargava, K.P., Gupta, M.B., Gupta, G.P. & Mitra, C.R. (1970). Anti-inflammatory activity of saponins and other natural products. Indian Journal of Medical Research 58: 724-30.

Bhatnagar, D. & Zeringue, H.J. (1993). Neem Leaf Extracts (Azadirachta Indica) inhibit biosynthesis in aspergillus flavus and A. parasiticus. Proceedings of the World Neem Conference, Bangalore, India. Feb: 24-8.

Bhattarai, N.K.(1992). Folk anthelminthic drugs of central Nepal. Int. J. Pharmacognocy, 30, No. 2: 145-50.

Bhide, N.K., Mehta, D.J., Lewis, R.A., & Attakar, W.W. (1958a). Toxicity of sodium nimbidinate. Indian Journal of Medical Science 12: 146-8.

Bhide, N.K., Mehta, D.J., & Lewis, R.A. (1958b). Diuretic action of sodium nimbidinate. Indian Journal of Medical Science 12: 141-5.

Bhowmick, B.N. & Choudharg, B.K. (1982). Anti-fungal activity of leaf extracts of medicinal plants on Alternaria alternata. Indian Botanical Reporter. 1: 164-5.

Boschitz, C., & Grunewald, J. (1994). The effect of NeemAzal on Aedes aegypti (Diptera: culicidae). Appl Parasitol, Nov;35(4): 251-6.

Brahmachari, H.D., & Sharma, C.B. (1958). Ascorbic acid (vitamin C) content of some fruits and vegetables in the desert areas of Rajasthan. Indian J of Applied Chemistry. 21(1): 39-40.

Bray, D.H., Warhurst, D.C., Connolly, J.D., O'Neill. M.J. & Phillipson, J.D. (1990). Plants as a source of antimalarial drugs. Part 7. Activity of some species of Meliaceae plants and their constituent limonoids. Phytotherapy Research. Vol. 4. No. 1: 29-35.

Caldwell, M. (1994). Blessed with resistance. Discover, December 1994: 46-48.

Castilla, V., Barquero, A.A., Mersich, S.E., & Coto, C.E. (1998). In-vitro anti-Junin virus activity of a peptide isolated from Melia azedarach L. leaves. Int J Antimicrob Agents. Apr; 10(1): 67-75.

Chakrabarty, M., Nath, A., Khasnobis, M., Konda, Y., Harigya, Y., & Komiyama, K. (1997). Carbazole alkaloids from Murraya koenigii. Phytochemistry. Oct; 46(4): 751-5.

Chakraborty, T., Podder, G. & Saha, J. (1984a). Phytochemical screening of medicinal plants for antidiabetic agents. Proc. Nat. Symp. on Applied Biotech. of Med. Aromatic Timber Yielding Plants. 12-13 Jan, 1984: 370-80.

Chakraborty, T. & Podder, G. (1984b). Herbal drugs in diabetes - Part I: Hypoglycemic activity of indigenous plants in Streptozotocin (STZ) induced diabetic rats. Journal of Inst. Chemists. (India) Vol. 56: 20-2.

Charles, V., & Charles, S.X. (1992). The use and efficacy of Azadirachta indica (neem) and Curcuma longa (Turmeric) in scabies. A pilot study. Trop Geogr Med. 44(1-2): 178-81.

Chary, M.P., Reddy, E.J.S. & Reddy, S.M. (1984). Screening of indigenous plants for their antifungal principle. Pesticides. 18 (4): 17-18.

Chatterjee, K.K. (1961). Treatment of cancer: a prelude. Indian Medical Record. 81: 101.

Chattopadhyay, R.R., Sarkar, S.K., Ganguly, S., & Banerjee, R.N. (1992a). Acute effects of Azadirachta indica leaves on some biochemical constituents of blood in rats. Science & Culture. 58(1&2): 39-40.

Chattopadhyay, R.R., Sarkar, S.K., Ganguly, S., & Banerjee, R.N. (1992b) Hepatoprotective activity of azadirachta indica leaves on paracetamol induced hepatic damage in rats. Indian Journal of Experimental Biology. 738-40.

Chattopadhyay, R.R., Sarkar, S.K., Ganguly, S., & Basu, T.K. (1994). A comparative evaluation of some anti-inflammatory agents of plant origin. Fitoterapia; 65(2): 146-8.

Chattopadhyay, R.R. (1996). Possible mechanism of antihyperglycemic effect of Azadirachta indica leaf extract: Part IV. Gen Pharmacol. Apr;27(3): 431-4.

Chattopadhyay, R.R. (1997). Effect of Azadirachta indica hydroalcoholic leaf extract on the cardiovascular system. Gen Pharmacol. Mar;28(3): 449-51.

Chattopadhyay, R.R. (1998). Possible biochemical mode of anti-inflammatory action of Azadirachta indica A. Juss. In rats. Indian J Exp Biol. Apr; 36(4): 418-20.

Chattopadhyay, R.R. (1999a). A comparative evaluation of some blood sugar lowering agents of plant origin. J Ethnopharmacol. Nov 30; 67(3):367-72.

Chattopadhyay, R.R. (1999b). Possible mechanism of antihyperglycemic effect of Azadirachta indica leaf extract: Part V. J Ethnopharmacol. Nov 30; 67(3):373-6.

Chiaki, N., Yoshio, K., Shigehiro, Y., Masaki, S., Yasuko, T. & Takeo, N. (1987). Polysaccharides as enhancers of antibody formation. Japan Kokai Tokkyo Koho JP 62,167729 (Cl.A61K31/715) : 6.

Chinnassamy, N., Harishankar, N., Kumar, P.U., & Rukmini, C. (1993). Toxicological studies on debitterized neem oil. Food Chem. Toxicol. Apr; 31(4): 297-301.

Chopra, I.C., Gupta, K.C. & Nazir, B.N. (1952). Preliminary study of antibacterial substances from Melia azadirachta. Indian Journal of Medical Research 40: 511-515.

Chopra, I.C. (1958) Proceedings of the Symposium on antibiotics. Council of Scientific and Industrial Research, India.: 43.

Chopra, R.N., Nayar, S.L. & Chopra, J.C. (1956). Glossary of Indian Medicinal Plants. C.S.I.R. Publications, New Dehli, India.: 31-2.

Chopra, R.N., Budhwar, R.L. and Ghosh, S. (1965). Poisonous plants of India. Indian Agricultural Research Institute, New Dehli. 1: 245.

Choudhary, D.N., Singh, J.N., Verma, S.K., & Singh, B.P. (1990). Antifertility effects of leaf extracts of some plants in male rats. Indian J Exp Biol. Aug; 28(8): 714-6

Cui, B., Chai, H., Constant, H.L., Santisuk, T., Reutrakul, V., Beecher, C.W., Farnsworth, N.R., Cordell, G.A., Pezzuto, J.M., & Kinghorn, A.D. (1998). Limonoids from Azadirachta excelsa. Phytochemistry. Apr;47(7): 1283-7.

Dakshinmurthi, K. (1954). The amino acids in the leaf of Azadirachta indica (Melia) Current Science (Bangalore), 23: 125-126.

Das, B.K., Mukherjee, S.C., Sahu, B.B., & Murjani, G. (1999). Neem (Azadirachta indica) extract as an antibacterial agent against fish pathogenic bacteria. Indian J Exp Biol. Nov; 37(11): 1097-100.

Das, N.G., Nath, D.R., Baruah, I., Talukdar, P.K., & Das, S.C. (1999). Field evaluation of herbal mosquito repellents. J Commun Dis. Dec; 31(4): 241-5.

Datur, J.F. (1977). Medicinal Plants of India and Pakistan. D.B. Taraporevala Sons, & Co., Bombay, India: 29-31.

De Azambuja, P., & Garcia, E.S. (1992). Effects of Azadirachtin on Rhodnius prolixus: immunity and Trypanosome interaction. Mem

Inst Oswaldo Cruz. 87 Suppl 5: 69-72.

Debelmas, A.M., & Hache, J. (1976). Etude pharmacologique de quelques plantes medicinales du Nepal. Toxicite aigure etude comportementale et action sur le systeme nerveux central. Planta medicinales et phylotherapie. 10: 128-38.

Descalzo, A.M., & Coto, C. (1989) Inhibition of the pseudoravies virus (Suis herpesvirus 1) by an antiviral agent isolated from the leaves of Melia azedarach. Rev Argent Microbiol. Jul-Dec; 21(3-4): 133-40.

Deshpande, V.Y., Mendulkar, K.N., & Sadre, N.L. (1980). Male antifertility activity of Azadirachta indica in mice. Journal of Postgraduate Medicine, Bombay. 26: 167-170.

Dey, A.C. (1980) Indian Medicinal Plants used in Ayurvedic Preparations. Bishen Singh Mahendra Pal Singh, Debra Dun, India: 165-166.

Dey, K.L., & Mair, W. (1973). The indigenous drugs of India. 2nd ed. Pama, Primlane, Chronica Botanica, New Dehli, India: 186-187.

Dhar, R., Zhang, K., Talwar, G.P., Garg, S., & Kumar, N. (1996). Effect of volatiles from neem and other natural products on gonotrophobic cycle and oviposition of Anopheles stephensi and An. culicifacies (Diptera; culicidae) J. Med Entomol, Mar; 33(2): 195-201.

Dhar, R., Zhang, K., Talwar, G.P., Garg, S., & Kumar, N. (1998). Inhibition of the growth and development of asexual and sexual stages of drug-sensitive and resistant strains of the human malaria parasite Plasmodium falciparum by Neem (Azadirachta indica) fractions. J Ethnopharmacol. May; 61(1): 31-9.

DiSepio, D., Chandrarantna, R.A., & Nagpal, S. (1999). Novel approaches for the treatment of psoriasis. Drug Discovery Today. May; 4(5): 222-231.

Dixit, V.P., Sinha, R., & Tank, R. (1986). Effect of neem seed oil on the blood glucose concentration of normal and alloxan diabetic rats. Journal of Ethnopharmacology. 17: 95-98.

Dunkel, F.V., Serugendo, A., Breene, W.M., & Sriharan, S. (1995). Influence of insecticidal plant materials used during storage on sensory attributes and instrumental hardness of dry edible beans (phaseolus vulgairs L.). Plant Foods Hum Nutr., Jul; 48(1): 1-16.

Dymock, W., Warden, C.J.H. & Hooper, D. (1890). Pharmacographia Indica. Vol. 1, Keegan Paul, Trench and Trubner & Co., London: 322-330.

Ekanem, O.J. (1978). Has Azadirachta indica (Dongoyaro) any antimalarial activity? Nigerian Medical Journal. 8: 8-10.

El-Hawary, Z.M., & Kholief, T.S. (1990). Biochemical studies on hypoglycemic agents (1) Effect of Azadirachta indica leaf extract. Archives of Pharmacal Research. 13(1): 108-112.

Elvin-Lewis, M. (1980). Plants used for teeth cleaning throughout the world. Journal of Preventative Dentistry. 6: 61-70.

Etkin, N.A., (1981). Hausa herbal pharmacopia: biomedical evaluation of commonly used medicines. Journal of Ethnopharmacology. 4: 75-98.

Fabry, W., Okemo, P., & Ansorg, R. (1998). Antibacterial activity of east African medicinal plants. J Ethnopharmacol. Feb; 60(1): 79-84.

Fabry, W., Okemo, P., & Ansorg, R. (1996). Fungistatic and fungicidal activity of east African medicinal plants. Mycoses. Jan-Feb; 39(1-2): 67-70.

Fujiwara, T., Takeda, T., Ogihara, Y., Shimizu, T., & Tomita, Y. (1982). Studies on the structure of polysaccharides from the bark of Melia azadirachta. Chem. Pharm. Bull. (Tokyo), 30: 4025-4030.

Fujiwara, T., Sugishita, E., Takeda, T., Ogihara, Y., Shimizu, M., Nomura, T., & Tomita, Y. (1984). Further studies on the structure of polysaccharides from the bark of the Melia azadirachta. Chemical and Pharmaceutical Bulletin 32: 1385-91

Gaitonde, B.B., & Sheth, U.K. (1957). Pharmacological studies of sodium nimbidinate. The Indian Journal of Medical Sciences. 156-61.

Gandhi, M., Lal, R., Sankaranarayanan, A., Banerjee, C.K., & Sharma, P.L. (1988). Acute toxicity study of the oil from Azadirachta indica seed (neem oil). Journal of Ethnopharmacology. 23: 39-51.

Garcia, E.S., Gonzales, M.S., & Azambuja, P. (1991). Effects of Azadirachtin in Rhodnius Prolixus: data and hypotheses. Mem. Inst. Oswaldo Cruz, Rio de Jenero, Vol. 86, Suppl. II, 107-111.

Garg, H.S., & Bhakuni, D.S. (1984). An isoprenylated flavanone from leaves of Azadirachta indica. Phytochemistry, 23: 2115-8.

Garg, H.S., Talwar, G.P., Upadhyay, S.N., Mittal, A., & Kapoor, S. (1993). Identification and characterization of the immunomodulatory fraction from neem-seed extract responsible for long-term antifertility activity after intrauterine administration. Proceedings of the World Neem Conference, Bangalore, India. Feb. 24-8.

Garg, H.S., Talwar, G.P., & Upadhyay, S.N. (1994). Comparison of extraction procedures on the immunocontraceptive activity of neem seed extracts. J Ethnopharmacol, Oct; 44(2): 87-92.

Garg, S., Taluja, V., Upadhyay, S.N., & Talwar, G.P. (1993). Studies on the contraceptive efficacy of Praneem polyherbal cream. Contraception. Dec; 48(6): 591-6.

Garg, S., Talwar, G.P., & Upadhyay, S.N. (1998) Immunocontraceptive activity guided fractionation and characterization of constituents of neem (Azadirachta indica) seed extracts. J Ethnopharmacol. Apr; 60(3): 235-46.

Garg, S., Singh, R., Kaur, R., Dhar, V. Talaja, V., & Talwar, G.P.(undated) Praneem polyherbal cream for contraception and genital tract infections. National Institute of Immunology.

Garg, G.P., Ogle, C.W., & Nigam, S.K. (1991). Mechanism of anti-ulcer action of leaves of the neem tree. Proc. 24th Indian Pharmacol. Soc. Conference, Ahmedabad, Gujarat, India, December 29-31, 1991: 40.

Garg, G.P., Nigam, S.K., & Ogle, C.W. (1993). The gastric antiulcer effects of the leaves of the neem tree. Planta Medica (59) 215-17.

Ghosh, B. (1987). Exploitation of Indian Plants in Homeopathic Medicine. Ind. J Forestry.10(3): 173-83.

Gonzalez, M.S., & Garcia, E.S. (1992). Effect of Azadirachtin on the development of Trypanosoma cruzi in different species of triatomine insect vectors: long-term and comparative studies. Journal of Invertebrate Pathology 60: 201-5.

Grant, I.F., Seegers, K., & Walanabe, I. (1984). Increasing biological nitrogen fixation in flooded rice using neem. In Proceedings of the 2nd International Neem Conference. Ravisch-holzhausen. West Germany, May 25, 1983: 493-506.

Guerrini V.H., & Kriticos C.M. (1998). Effects of azadirachtin on Ctenocephalides felis in the dog and the cat.Vet Parasitol, 74(2-4): 289-97.

Halde, U.K., & Joshi, V. (1986). Dantadhavanakashta and amylase activity. Nagarjun, Vol 29(6), 9-10.

Hanifa Moursi, S.A., & Al-Khatib, I.M. (1984). Effects of Melia azedarach fruits on gipsing-restraint stress-induced ulcers in rats. Jpn J Pharmacol. Dec; 36(4): 527-33.

Hare, W.R., Schutzman, H., Lee, B.R., & Knight, M.W. (1997). Chinaberry poisoning in two dogs. J Am Vet Med Assoc. Jun 1;210(11): 1638-40.

Hartwell, J.L. (1983). Plants used against cancer, a survey. Quarterman (Lawrence, MA,) 33: 181.

Ibrahim, I.A., Khalid, S.A., Omer, S.A., & Adam, S.E.I. (1992). On the toxicology of azadirachta indica leaves. Journal of Ethnopharmacology. 35. 267-73.

Itokawa, H., Qiao, Z.S., Hirobe, C., & Takeya, K. (1995). Cytotoxic limonoids and tetranortriterpenoids from Melia azedarach. Chem Pharm Bull (Tokyo),. Jul; 43(7): 1171-5.

Iwu, M.M., Obidoa, O., & Anazodo, M. (1986). Biochemical mechanism of the antimalarial activity of Azadirachta indica leaf extract. Pharmacological Res Communications. 18: 81-91.

Jaiswal, A.K., Bhattacharya, S.K., & Acharya, S.B. (1994). Anxiolytic activity of Azadirachta indica leaf extract in rats. Indian Journal of Experimental Biology. 32: 489-91.

Jayaweera, D.M.A. (1982). Medicinal Plants (Indigenous and Exotic) used in Ceylon, Part IV. The National Science Council of Sri Lanka, Colombo: 52-3.

Jones, I.W., Denholm, A.A., Ley, S.V., Lovell, H., Wood, A., & Sinden, R.E. (1994). Sexual development of malaria parasites is inhibited in vitro by neem extract and its semi-synthetic analogues. FEMS Microbiol Lett. Jul. 15;120(3): 267-73.

Jongen, W.M.F., & Koeman, J.H. (1983). Mutagenicity testing of two tropical plant materials with pesticidal potential in Salmonella typhimurium: Phytobacca dodecandra berries and oil from seeds of Azadirachta indica. Environmental Mutagenesis 5: 687-694.

Joshi, A.R., Ahmed, R.N., Pathan, K.M., & Manivannan, B. (1996). Effects of Azadirachta indica leaves on testis and its recovery in albino rats. Indian J Exp Bio. Nov; 34(11): 1091-4.

Juneja, S.C., & Williams, R.S. (1993). Mouse sperm-egg interaction in vitro in the presence of neem oil. (unpublished).

Juneja, S.C., Pfeifer, T., Williams, R.S., & Chegini, N. (1994). Neem Oil inhibits two-cell embryo development and trophectoderm attachment and proliferation in vitro. J Assist Reprod Genet. Sept; 11(8): 419-27.

Kasutri, M., Ahmed, R.N., Pathan, K.M., Shaikh, P.D., & Manivannan, B. (1997) Effects of Azadirachta indica leaves on the seminal vesicles and ventral prostate in albino rats. Indian J Physiol Pharmacol. Jul; 41(3): 234-40.

Kaushic, C., & Upadhyay, S. (1995). Mode of long term antifertility of intrauterine neem treatment (IUNT). Contraception. Mar; 51(3): 203-7.

Kehra, N.D., & Nagi, S.S. (1949). Neem leaves as a feed for livestock. Current Science (Bangalore), 18: 325.

Ketkar, C.M. (1976). Utilization of Neem (azadirachta indica) J. and its by-products. Final Technical Report. Directorate of Non-edible Oils and Soap Industry. Khadi and Village Industries Commission. 1st ed. Nana Dengle Sadhana Press, Poona, India.

Khalid, S.A., Farouk, A., Geary, T.G., & Jensen, J.B. (1986). Potential antimalarial candidates from African plants. An in vitro approach using Plasmodium falciparum. Journal of Ethnopharmacology.

15: 201-209.

Khalid, S.A., Duddeck, H., & Gonzalez-Sierra, M. (1989a). Gedunin is molecule responsible for anti-malarial activity, found in bark of neem tree. Journal of Natural Products, Sep-Oct. 52(5): 922-927.

Khalid, S.A., Duddeck, H., & Gonzalez-Sierra, M. (1989b) Isolation and characterization of an anti-malarial agent of the neem tree (Azadirachta indica). Journal of Natural Products. 52[2] 922-926.

Khan, B.M., Abraham, A., & Leelamma, S. (1995). Hypoglycemic action of Murraya koenigii (curry leaf) and Brassica juncea (mustard): mechanism of action. Indian J Biochem Biophys. Apr; 32(2): 106-8.

Khan, B.M., Abraham, A., & Leelamma, S. (1996a). Role of Murraya koenigii (curry leaf) and Brassica juncea (Mustard) in lioid peroxidation). Indian J Physiol Pharmacol. Apr; 40(2): 155-8.

Khan, B.M., Abraham, A., & Leelamma, S. (1996b). Biochemical response in rats to the addition of curry leaf (Murraya koenigii) and mustard seeds (Brassica juncea) to the diet. Jun; 49(4): 295-9.

Khan, B.M., Abraham, A., & Leelamma, S. (1997). Anti-oxidant effects of curry leaf, Murraya koenigii and mustard seeds, Brassica juncea in rats fed with high fat diet. Indian J Exp Biol. Feb; 35(2): 148-50.

Khan, M., & Wassilew, S.W. (1987). The effects of raw material from the neem tree, neem oil and neem extracts on fungi pathogenic to humans. In Proceedings of the 3rd International Neem Conference, Nairobi, Kenya, July 10: 685-650.

Khan, M., Schneider, B., Wassilew, S.W., & Splanemann, V. (1988). Petrol ether leaf extract proved effective as an antimycotic, possibly due to quercetins (a flavonoid) in the leaves. Z Hautkr. Jun 15;63(6): 499-502.

Khan, M., Plempei, M., & Wassilew, S.W. (1991). The effect of petrol ether - extract of neem leaves on fungi pathogenic to humans in vitro and in vivo. Recent Advances in Medicinal, Aromatic and Spice Crops. Vol. I: 269-72.

Khan, M.M., Khan, M., & Saxena, S.K. (1974). Rhizospere fungi and nematodes of egg plant as influenced by oil cake amendments. Indian Phytopathol. 27: 480-484.

Khanna, K.K., & Chandra, S. (1972). Antifungal activity of some plant extracts. Proceedings of the National Academy of Science, India. 42 (B) III.

Khanna, N., Goswami, M., Sen, P., & Ray, A. (1995). Antinociceptive action of Azadirachta indica (neem) in mice: possible mechanisms involved. Indian J Exp Biol. Nov; 33(11): 848-50.

Khare, A.K., Srivastava, M.C., Sharma, M.K., & Tewari, J.P. (1984). Antifertility activity of neem oil in rabbits and rats. Probe. 23: 90-3.

Khare, N.V. (1990). Azadirachta indica (neem): panchabhautika aspect in relation to chikitsa. Deerghayu International, Vol. VI: 6-8.

Khattak, S.G., Gilani, S.N., & Ikram, M. (1985) Anti-pyretic studies on some indigenous Pakistani medicinal plants. Journal of Ethnopharmacology 14: 45-51.

Kher, A., & Chauraisia, S.C. (1977) Anti-fungal activity of essential oils of three medicinal plants. Indian Drugs. 15: 41-2.

Khosla, P., Bhanwra, S., Singh, J., Seth, S., & Srivastava, R.K. (2000) A study of hypoglycemic effects of Azadirachta indica (Neem) in normal and alloxin diabetic rabbits. Indian J Physiol Pharmacol. Jan; 44(1): 69-74.

Kim, M., Kim, S.K., Park, B.N., Lee, K.H., Min, G.H., Seoh, J.Y., Park, C.G., Hwang, E.S., Cha, C.Y., & Kook, Y.H. (1999). Antiviral effects of 28-deacetylsendanin on herpes simplex virus-1 replication. Antiviral Res. Sept; 43(2): 103-12.

Koga, Y., Yoshida, I., Kimura, A., Yoshino, M., Yamashita, F., & Sinniah, D. (1987). Inhibition of mitochondrial functions by margosa oil: possible implications of the pathogenesis of Reye's syndrome. Pediatric Research 22: 184-7.

Koley, K.M., & Lal, J., (1994). Pharmacological effects of Azadirachta indica (neem) leaf extract on the ECG and blood pressure of rat. Indian Journal of Physical Pharmacology. Jul; 38(3): 223-5.

Komolafe, O.O., Anyabuike, A.O., & Obaseki, A.O. (1988). The possible role of mixed-function oxidases in the hepatobilary toxicity of Azadirachta indica. Fitoterapia, Vol. LIX, No. 2: 109-13.

Koner, B.C., Banerjee, B.D., & Ray, A. (1997). Effects of stress on gamma glutamyl transpeptidase (GGT) activity in lymphoid system of rats. Indian J Exp Biol. Mar; 35(3): 222-4.

Koo, J., & Lebwohl, M. (1999). Duration of remission of psoriasis therapies. J Am Acad Dermatol. Jul; 41(1): 51-9.

Koul, O., Isman, M.B., & Ketkar, C.M. (1990). Properties and uses of neem. Can. J. Bot. 68: 1-11.

Kroes, B.H., Van den Berg, A.J.J., Labadie, R.P., Abeysekera, A.M., & de Silva, K.T.D. (1993). Impact of the preparation process on immunomodulatory activities of the Ayurvedic drug Nimba arishta. Phytochemistry Research. 7(1): 35-40.

Kusamran, W.R., Ratanavila, A., & Tepsuwan, A. (1998) Effects of neem flowers, Thai and Chinese bitter gourd fruits and sweet basil leaves on hepatic monooxygenases and glutathione S-transferase activities, and in vitro metabolic activation of chemical carcinogens in rats. Food Chem Toxicol. Jun; 36(6): 475-84.

Labadie, R.P., van der Nat, J.M., Simons, J.M., Kroes, B.H., Kosasi, S., van den Berg, A.J.J., 't Hart, L.A., van der Sluis, W.G., Abeysekera, A., Bamunuarachchi, A., & De Salva, K.T.D., (1989). An ethnopharmacognostic approach to the search for immunomodulators of plant origin. Planta Medica. 55: 339-48.

Lal, R., Sankaranarayanan, A., Mathur, V.S., & Sharma, P.L. (1985). Antifertility effect of neem oil in female albino rats by intravaginal and oral routes. Indian Journal of Medical Research. 83: 89 - 92.

Lal, R., Gandhi, M., Sankaranarayanan, A., Mathur, V.S., & Sharma, P.L. (1987) Antifertility effect of Azadirachta indica oil administered per os to female albino rats on selected days of pregnancy. Fitoterapia. 58: 239-42.

Lans, C., & Brown,G. (1998). Ethnoveterinary medicines used for ruminants in Trinidad and Tobago. Prev Vet Med. Jun 1; 35(3): 149-63.

Larson, R.O. (1987) Development of Margosan-O, a pesticide from neem seed. In Proceedings of the 3rd International Neem Conference, Nairobi, Kenya, July 10, 1986: 243-50.

Larson, R.O. (1993). Neem: the tree for today, tomorrow and beyond. Presentation to the American Chemical Society Annual Meeting. March 31, 1993.

Lavie, D., Levy, E.C., & Jain, M.K. (1971). Limonoids of biogenetic interest from Melia azadirachta. Tetrahedron 27: 3927-39.

Ley, S.V. (1990). Synthesis of antifeedants for insects: novel behavior-modifying chemicals from plants. Ciba Found Symp 154:80-7; discussion 87-98.

Liu, T.P.S., Spons, P., & Nasr, M.E. Integrated bee diseases and parasite management. Project Nbr. 380-1352-8102. University of Alberta, Faculty of Agriculture and Forestry.

Lorenz, H.K.P., (1976). Neem tree bark extract in the treatment of inflammatory stomatitis. Zahnaerztl. Proxis 8: 1-4.

Luscombe, D.K., & Taha, S.A. (1974). Pharmacological studies on the leaves of Azadirachta indica. Journal of Pharmacy and Pharmacology. 26: Suppl: 110-111.

MacKinnon, S., Durst, T., Arnason, J.T., Angerhofer, C., Pezzuto, J., Sanchez-Vindas, P.E., Poveda, L.J., & Gbeassor, M. (1997). Antimalarial activity of tropical Meliaceae extracts and gedunin derivatives. J Nat Prod. Apr; 60(4): 336-41.

Maramorosch, K. (1991). Current status of neem pesticides and by-products. Recent advances in Medicinal, Aromatic & Spice Crops, Vol. 1:23-9.

Mateenuddin, M., Kharaitkin, K.K., Mendulkar, K.N., & Sadre, N.L. (1986). Assessment of estrogenicity of neem (Azadirachta indica) leaf extracts in rats. Indian Journal of Physiology and Pharmacology 30: 118-20.

Melathopoulos, A.P., Winston, M.L., Whittington, R., Smith, T., Lindberg, C., Mukai, A., & Moore, M. (2000). Comparative laboratory toxicity of neem pesticides to honey bees (Hymenoptera: Apidae), their mite parasites Varroa jacobsoni (Acari: Varroidae) and Acarapis woodi (Acari: Tarsonemidae), and brood pathogens Paenibacillus larvae and Ascophaera apis. J Econ Entomol. Apr; 93(2): 199-209

Miller, J.A., & Chamberlain, W.F., (1989). Azadirachtin as a larvicide against the horn fly, stable fly, and house fly (Diptera: Muscidae). J Econ Entomol. Oct; 82(5): 1375-8.

Mishra, A.K., Singh, N., & Sharma, V.P. (1995). Use of neem oil as a mosquito repellent in tribal villages of Mandla district, Mandhya Pradesh. Indian J Malariol. Sept; 32(3): 99-103.

Mitra, C.R. (1961). Some important characteristics of neem oil and its standardization. Indian Oil Seeds Journal. Vol. 3: 204-7

Mitra, C.R., & Misra, P.S. (1967). Amino acids of processed seed meal proteins. Journal of Agricultural Food Chemistry 15: 697-700.

Mukherjee, S., & Talwar, G.P. (1996a) Termination of pregnancy in rodents by oral administration of Praneem, a purified neem seed extract. Am J Reprod Immunol, Jan; 35(1): 51-6.

Mukherjee, S., Lohiya, N.K., Pal, R., Sharma, M.G., & Talwar, G.P. (1996b). Purified neem (Azadirachta indica) seed extracts (Praneem) abrogate pregnancy in primates. Contraception. Jun; 53(6): 375-8.

Mukherjee, S., Garg, S., & Talwar, G.P. (1999). Early post implantation contraceptive effects of a purified fraction of neem (Azadirachta indica) seeds, given orally in rats; possible mechanisms involved. J-Ethnopharmacol. Nov. 30; 67(3): 287-96.

Mulla, M.S., & Su, T.(1999). Activity and biological effects of neem products against arthropods of medicinal and veterinary importance. J Am Mosq Control Assoc. Jun; 15(20: 133-52.

Murty, K.S., Rao, D.N., Rao, D.K., & Murty, L.B.G. (1978). A preliminary study on the hypoglycemic and antihyperglycemic effects of Azadirachta indica. Indian Journal of Pharmacology. 10: 247-50.

Murthy, S.P., & Sirsi, M. (1958a). Pharmacological studies on Melia azadirachta. L. Indian Journal of Physiological Pharmacology. 2: 387-396.

Murthy, S.P., & Sirsi, M. (1958b). Pharmacological studies on Melia azadirachta. L. Indian Journal of Physiological Pharmacology. 2: 456-61.

Nadkarni, K.M., & Nadkarni, A.K. (1954). Indian materia medica. 3rd ed. Vol. 1. Popular Book Depot, Bombay, India: 776-84.

Nagpal, B.N., Srivastava, A., & Sharma, V.P. (1995). Control of mosquitoes breeding using wood scrapings treated with neem oil. Indian J. Malariol. Jun; 32(2): 64-9.

Nair, P.R., Namboodiri, M.N.S., Madhavikutty, P., & Prabhakaran, V.A. (1987). Clinical evaluation of Ayurvedic preparations in vitiligo. J. Res. Ayur. Sid. 8(1-2) pp. 30-8.

Narayan, D.S. (1965). The antifungal activity of neem oil and its constituents. Mediscope. Vol. VIII, 6: 323-6.

Narayan, D.S. (1969). Anti pyretic effect of neem oil and its constituents. Mediscope. Vol. XII. 12: 25-27.

Narayan, D.S. (1978). Effect of neem oil and its constituents on cotton pellet inflammation. Mediscope. Vol. XX, 12: 273-74.

National Research Council (1992). Neem: A Tree For Solving Global Problems. National Academy Press, Washington, D.C.

Nayak, B.R., & Pattabiraman, T.N. (1978). Studies on plant gums: part III-isolation & characterization of a glycopeptide from neem (azadirachta indica) gum pronase digestion. Indian Journal of Biochemistry & Biophysics, Vol. 15: 449-55.

Ndumu, P.A., George, J.B., & Choudhury, M.K. (1999). Toxicity of neem seed oil (Azadirachta indica) against the larvae of amblyomma variegatum a three-host tick in cattle. Phytother Res. Sept; 13(6): 532-4.

Njiro, S.M., & Kofi-Tsekpo, M.W. (1999). Effect of an aqueous extract of Azadirachta indica on the immune response in mice. Onderstepoort J Vet Res. Mar;66(1): 59-62.

Obaseki, A.O, Adeyi, O., & Anyabuike, C. (1985). Some serum enzyme levels as marks of possible acute effects of the aqueous extract of Azadirachta indica on membranes in vitro. Fitoterapia. 56: 111-15.

Obaseki, A.O., & Jegede-Fadunsin, H.A. (1986). The antimalarial activity of Azadirachta indica. Fitoterapia 57: 247-51.

Obih, P.O., & Makinde, J.M. (1985). Effect of Azadirachta indica on Plasmodium berghei berghei in mice. African Journal of Medicine and Medical Sciences 14: 51-4.

Okpako, D.T. (1977). Prostaglandin synthetase inhibitory effect of Azadirachta indica. Journal of West African Science Association. 22: 45-7.

Okpanyi, S.N., & Ezeukwa, G.C. (1981). Anti-inflammatory and anti-pyretic actions of Azadirachta indica, Plant Med. 41: 34-9.

Osula, F.O.U., & Okwuosa, V.N. (1993). Toxicity of azadirachta indica to freshwater snails and fish, with reference to the physicochemical factor on potency. Appl. Parasitol. 34: 63-8.

Palsson, K., & Jaenson, T.G. (1999). Plant products used as mosquito repellents in Guinea Bissau, West Africa. Acta Trop. Jan 15; 72(1):39-52.

Pandya, K.K., Mangalan, S., Champaneri, D.K., Motwani, K.T., Atreya, A., Patel, R.B., & Chakravarthy, B.K. (1990). Antimicrobial efficacy of melicon V: a veterinary herbal antiseptic ointment. Indian Drugs, 28(6): 255-8.

Paranjapo, M.H., & Paranjapo, M.M. (1993). Use of neem oil (azadirachta indica) suppositories as contraceptive. Proceedings of the World Neem Conference, Bangalore, India. Feb: 24-8.

Parashar, K.S., Prasad, R.P., Sharma, S.N., & Singh, S. (1980). Efficiency of urea, nitrification inhibitor treated urea and slow release nitrogen fertilizers for sugarcane. Z. Pflanzenernaehr. Dueng, Bodenbed. 143: 262-7.

Parshad, O., Singh, P., Gardner, M. Fletcher, C., Rickards, E., & Choo-Kank, E. (1994). Effect of aqueous neem (Azadirachta indica) extract on testosterone and other blood constituents in male rats. West Indian Medical Journal, Sep; 43(3): 71-4.

Patel, M.S. (1965). Development of minor and non-edible oils. Report of the special subcommittee. Indian Oil Seeds Committee. Hyderabad, India: 17-27.

Patel, R.P., & Trivedi, B.M. (1962). The in vitro antibacterial activity of some medicinal oils. Indian Journal of Medical Research 50: 218-22.

Patel, V.K., & Venkatakrishna-Blatt, H.(1988). Folklore therapeutic indigenous plants in periodontal disorders in India (review experimental and clinical approach) Int J Clin Pharmacol Ther Toxicol. Apr; 26(4): 176-84.

Pertoldi, F., D'Orlando, L., & Mercante, W.P. (1999). Acute salicylate intoxication after trancutaneous absorption. Minerva Anestesiol. Jul-Aug; 65(7-8): 571-3.

Pettit, G.R., Barton, H.D.R., Herald, G.L., Polonsky, J., Schmidt, J.M., & Conolly, J.D. (1983). Evaluation of limonoids against murine P-388 lymphocytic leukemia cell line. J. Nat. Prod. 46: 379-90.

Pillai, N.R., Suganthan, D., Seshadri, C., & Santhakumari, G. (1978a). Anti-gastric ulcer activity of nimbidin. Indian Journal of Medical Research. 68: 169-175.

Pillai, N.R., Suganthan, D., Seshadri, C. and Santhakumari, G. (1978b). Analgesic and anti-pyretic actions of nimbidin. Bull. Med. Ethno. Bot. Res. 1: 393-400.

Pillai, N.R., Suganthan, D., & Santhakumari, G. (1980). Analgesic and anti-pyretic actions of nimbidin. Bull. Med. Ethno. Bot. Res. 1: 393-400.

Pillai, N.R., & Santhakumari, G. (1981a) Anti-arthritic and anti-inflammatory actions of nimbidin. Planta Medica 43:59-63.

Pillai, N.R., & Santhakumari, G. (1981b) Hypoglycemic activity of Melia azadirachta Linn (Neem). Indian Journal of Medical Research 74: 931-3.

Pillai, N.R., & Santhakumari, G. (1984a) Toxicity studies on nimbidin, a potential anti-ulcer drug. Planta Medica 50: 146-8.

Pillai, N.R., & Santhakumari, G. (1984b) Effects of nimbidin on acute and chronic gastro-duodenal ulcer models in experimental animals. Planta Medica 50: 143-6.

Pillai, N.R., & Santhakumari, G. (1984c). Some pharmacological actions of 'nimbidin' - a bitter principle of azadirachta indica - A juss. (neem). Ancient Science of Life. Vol IV, (2): 88 - 95.

Polasa, K., & Rukmini, C. (1987). Mutagenicity tests of cashew nut shell liquid, rice-bran oil and other vegetable oils using the salmonella typhimurium microsome system. Fd. Chem. Toxic. Vol. 25, (10): 763-6.

Prakash, A.O., Tewari, R.K., & Mathur, R. (1988). Non-hormonal post-coital contraceptive action of neem oil in rats. Journal of Ethnopharmacology. 23: 53-9.

Prakash, A.O., Mishra, A., Metha, H., & Mathur, R. (1991). Effect of ethanolic extract of Azadirachta indica seeds on organs in female rats. Fitoterapia. Vol. LXII. (2): 99-105.

Prasad, H.C., Mazumder, R., & Chakraborty, R. (1993). Research on two medicinal plants from 'Ayurvedic' system of medicine Azadirachta indica A juss and Melia Azadirach Linn. Their past, present and future. Deerghayu International. July - Sept.

Prasad, R., Singh, S., Saxena, V.S., & Devkumar, C. (1999). Coating of prilled urea with neem (Azadirachta indica juss) oil for efficient nitrogen use in rice. Naturwissenschaften. Nov; 86(11): 538-9.

Puri, H.S. (1993). Therapeutic uses of neem. (unpublished)

Quadri, S.S.H., Usha, G., & Jabeen, K. (1984). Sub-acute dermal toxicity of neemrich-100 (Tech) to rats. Int. Pest Control. 26: 18-20.

Rai, A., & Sethi, M.S. (1972). Screening of some plants for their activity against vaccinia and fowl-pox viruses. Indian J. of Animal Science. 42: 1066-70.

Rai, M.K. (1988). In-vitro sensitivity of microsporum nanum to some plant extracts. Indian Drugs, 25(12): 521-3.

Rai, M.K. (1996). In vitro evaluation of medicinal plant extracts against Pestalotiopsis mangifarae. Hindustan Antibiot Bull. Feb-Nov; 38(1-4): 53-6.

Rajasekbaran, S., Pillai, N.G.K.P., Kurup, P.B., Pillai, K.G.B., & Nair, C.P.R. (1980). Effects of nimbidin in psoriasis - a case report. Journal of Res. Ayurveda. 52-8.

Ramakrishna, G., Prasad, N.B.L., & Azeemoddin, G. (1993). Cold processing neem seed. JNTU, Oil Technological Research Institute. Proceedings of the World Neem Conference, Bangalore, India. Feb. 24 - 28, 1993.

Rao, A.D., Devi, K.N., & Thyagaraju, K. (1998). Isolation of antioxidant principle from Azadirachta seed kernels: determination of its role on plant lipoxygenases. J Enzyme Inhib. 14(1): 85-96.

Rao, A.R., Kumar, S.S.U., Paramasivam, T.B., Kamalakshi, S., Parashuraman, A.R., & Shantha, M. (1969). Study of antiviral activity of tender leaves of margosa tree (Melia azadirachta) on vaccinia and variola virus - A preliminary report. Indian Journal of Medical Research 57: 495-502.

Rao, D.R., Ruben, R., & Nagasampazi, B.A. (1995). Development of combined use of neem (Azadirachta indica) and water management for the control of culicine mosquitoes in rice fields. Med Vet Entomol. Jan; 9(1): 25-33.

Rao, D.R., Reuben, R., Gitanjali, Y., & Srimannarayana, G. (1988). Evaluation of four azadirachtin rich fractions from neem, Azadirachta indica A. Jus. (family:meliaceae) as mosquito larvicides. Indian Journal of Malariology, Vol. 25, Dec: 67-72.

Rao, D.V.K., Singh, K., Chabra, P.C., & Ramanujilu, G. (1986). In vitro antibacterial activity of neem oil. Indian Journal of Medical Research 84: 314-16.

Ray, A. (1992). Anti-stress effects of some indigenous drugs: Role of Dopamine. International Seminar-Traditional Medicine, Nov; (99): 7-9.

Ray, A., Banerjee, B.D., & Sen, P. (1996). Modulation of humoral and cell mediated immune responses by Azadirachta indica (Neem) in mice. Indian-j-Exp-Biol. Jul; 34(7): 698-701.

Rembold, H.(undated), Biochemistry of neem.

Riar, S.S, Bardham, J., Thomas, P., Kain, A.K., & Parshad, R. (1988). Mechanism of anti-fertility action of neem oil. Indian Journal of Medical Research. 88: 339-42.

Riar, S.S., Devakumar, C., Sawhney, R.C., Ilavazhagan, G., Bardhan, J., Kain, A.K., Thomas, P., Singh, R., Singh, B. & Parshad, R. (1991). Antifertility activity of volatile fraction of neem oil. Contraception, Sep; 44(3): 319-26.

Riar, S.S., Sawhney, R.C., Llavazhagan, G., Roy, J.B., Kain, A.K., Thomas, P., Singh, R, Singh, B., Devakumar, C. Singh, M., & Sawhney, R.C. (1993) Neem as a contraceptive. Proceedings of the World Neem Conference, Bangalore, India. Feb. 24-28, 1993.

Rochanakij, S., Thebtaranonth, Y., Yanjai, C., & Yutharong, Y. (1985). Nimbolide, a constituent of Azadirachta indica inhibits Plasmodium falciparum in culture. Southeast Asian Journal of Tropical Medicine and Public Health 16: 66-72.

Rojanapo, W., Suwanno, S., Somjaree, R., Glinsukon, T., & Thebtaranonth, Y. (1985). Mutagenic and antibacterial activity testing of nimbolide and nimbic acid. Journal of the Scientific Society of Thailand. 11: 177-88.

Sadekar, R.D., Kolte, A.Y., Barmase, B.S., & Desai, V.F. (1998). Immunopotentiating effects of Azadirachta indica (Neem) dry leaves powder in broilers, naturally infected with IBD virus. Indian J Exp Biol. Nov; 36(11): 1151-3.

Sadre, N.L., Deshpande, V.Y., Mendulkar, K.N., & Nandal, D.H. (1984). Male anti-fertility of Azadirachta indica in different species. In Proceedings of the 2nd International Neem Conference, Rauischholzhausen, W. Germany, May 25, 1983: 473-82.

SaiRam, M., Sharma, S.K., Ilavazhagan, G., Kumar, D., & Selvamurthy, W. (1997). Immunomodulatory effects of MIM-76, a volatile fraction from Neem oil. J Ethnopharmacol. Jan; 55(2): 133-9.

SaiRam, M., Ilavazhagan, G., Sharma, S.K., Dhanraj, S.A., Suresh, B., Parida, M.M., Jana, A.M., Devendra, K., & Selvamurthy, W. (2000). Antimicrobial activity of a new vaginal contraceptive NIM-76 from neem oil (Azadirachta indica.J Ethnopharmacol. Aug;1(71)(3): 377-82.

Sambrook, P.N. (2000). Corticosteroid osteoporosis. Z Rheumatol. 59 Suppl 1: 45-7.

Samudraiwar, D.L., & Garg, A.N. (1996). Minor and trace elemental determination in the Indian herbal and other medicinal preparations. Biol Trace Elem Res. Aug; 54(2): 113-21.

Sankaram, A.V.B., Murthy, M.M., Bhaskaraiah, K., Subramanyam, M., Sultana, N., Sharma, H.C., Leuschnwer, K., Ramprasad, G., Sitaramaiah, S., Rukmini, C., & Rao, P.U. (1987) Chemistry, biological activity and utilization aspects of some promising neem extractives. In Proceedings of the 3rd International Neem Conference, Nairobi, Kenya, July 10, 1986: 127-148.

Santhoshumari, K.S., & Devi, K.S. (1990) Hypoglycemic effect of a few medicinal plants. Ancient Science of Life, 9(4): 221-3.

Saraf, A.P., & Joglekar, V.K. (1993). Study of effect of "Karnim" in patients of non insulin dependent diabetes mellitus.

Sawanobori, H. (1978). Melia azadirachta (neem) extracts for skin cosmetics. Chem. Abstr., 88: 11747s.

Saxena, R.C., Khan, Z.R., & Bajet, N.B. (1985). Neem seed derivatives for preventing rice tungro virus transmission by the green leafhopper. Nephot ettx Vikescens (Distant) Phil. Phyto Pathol. 21: 88-102.

Saxena, R.C. (undated), Scope of neem for developing countries.

Schmutterer, H., Instituit fur Phytopathologie und Augewandte Zoologie, Justis-Liebig-Universitat, Ludwigstrasse 23, 6300 Giessen. As cited in "Neem - A Tree for Solving Global Problems", National Academy Press, 1992: 62.

Schmutterer, H. and Ascher, K.R.S. (Eds.) (1985) Natural pesticides from the neem tree and other tropical plants. In Proceedings of the 3rd International Neem Conference. Nairobi, Kenya July 10, 1986.

Schneider, B.H., (1986). The effect of neem leaf extracts on Epilachna varivestis and Staphylococcus aureas. 3rd International Neem Conference, Nairobi, Kenya, 73.

Sen, P., Mediratta, P.K., & Ray, A. (1992) Effects of Azadirachta indica A Juss on some biochemical, immunological and visceral parameters in normal and stressed rats. Indian J Exp Biol, Dec; 30(12): 1170-5.

Sen, P., Mediratta, P., Ray, A., & Puri, S. (1993). An experimental evaluation of azadirachta indica (neem) in normal and stressed rats and adaptogenic effects.. Proceedings of the World Neem Conference, Bangalore, India. Feb. 24-28, 1993.

Shah, M.P., Sheth, U.K., Bhide, N.K., & Shah, M.J. (1958). Clinical trials with parenteral sodium nimbidinate, a new diuretic. Indian Journal of Medical Science. 12: 150-3.

Sharma, J.D., Jha, R.K., Gupta, I., Jain, P., & Dixit, V.P. (1987). Antiandrogenic properties of neem seed oil (Azadirachta indica.) in male rat and rabbit. Ancient Science of Life. Vol. VII.(1) 30-8.

Sharma, M.K., Khare, A.K., & Feroz, H. (1983). Effect of neem oil on blood levels of normal, hyperglycemic and diabetic animals. Nagarjun 26: 247-50.

Sharma, U.N., & Saksena, K.P. (1959a). Sodium nimbidinate in vitro study of its spermicidal action. Indian Journal of Medical Science. 13: 1038-41.

Sharma, U.N., & Saksena, K.P. (1959b). Spermicidal activity of sodium nimbidinate. Indian Journal of Medical Science. 47: 322-5.

Sharma, V.P., & Ansara, M.A., Personal protection from mosquitoes (Diptera culicidae) by burning neem oil in kerosene. Malaria Research Centre (ICMR) Delhi, India.

Sharma, V.P., Ansara, M.A., & Razdan, R.K., (1993a). Mosquito repellent action of neem (Azadirachta indica) oil. J. Am. Mosq Control Assoc. Sep; 9(3): 359-60.

Sharma, V.P., Nagpal, B.N., & Srivastava, A., (1993b) Effectiveness of neem oil mats in repelling mosquitoes. Transactions of the Royal Society of Tropical Medicine and Hygiene.87.626.

Sharma, V.P., & Dhiman, R.C., (1993c). Neem oil as a sand fly (Diptera psychodidae) repellent. J. Am. Mosq Control Assoc. Sep; 9(3): 359-60.

Shimizu, M., Sudo, T., Nomura, T. (1985a). Neem Bark Extracts. U.S. Patent 4,515,785.

Shimizu, M., Sudo, T., Nomura, T. (1985b). Hot-water extracts of neem bark. U.S. Patent 4,537,774.

Shukla, R. Singh, S., & Bhandari, C.R. (1973). Preliminary clinical trials on antidiabetic actions of Azadirachta indica. Medicine and Surgery 13: 11-12.

Siddiqui, S., & Mitra, C.R. (1945) Utilization of nim oil and its bitter constituents (nimbidin series) in the pharmaceutical industry. Journal of Scientific and Industrial Research. 4: 5-10.

Siddiqui, S., Faizi, S., Siddiqui, B.S., & Ghiasuddin (1992). Constituents of Azadirachta indica: isolation and structure elucidation of a new antibacterial tetranortriterpenoid, mahmoodin, and a new protolimonoid, naheedin. J Nat Prod. Mar; 55(3): 303-10.

Simons, N.J. (1981). Innovative methods of control of insect transmitted viral disease. In Vector of disease agents: Interaction with plants, animals and men. Edited by J.K. McKelvey, J., K. Maramor and B.F. Eldnge. New York 169-78.

Singh, H. (1988). Ethno biological treatment of piles by Bhoxas of Utter Pradesh. Ancient Science of Life. Vol. VIII, (2), 167-70.

Singh, N., Misra, N., Singh, S.P., & Kohli, R.P. (1979). Melia azadirachta in some common skin disorders, a clinical evaluation. Antiseptic. 76: 677-79.

Singh, N., Nath, R., Singh, S.P., & Kohli, R.P. (1980). Clinical evaluation of anthelminthic activity of Melia azadirachta. Antiseptic. 77: 739-41.

Singh, N., & Sastry, M.S. (1981). Anti-microbial activity of neem oil. Indian Journal of Pharmacology. 13: 102.

Singh, P.P., Junnarkar, A.Y., Reddi, G.S., & Singh, K.V. (1987). Azadirachta indica: neuro-psychopharmacological and anti-microbial studies. Fitoterapia 58: 235-38.

Sinha, K.C., Riar, S.S., Tiwary, R.S., Dhawan, A.K., Bardhan, J., Thomas, P., Kain, A.K., & Jain, R.K. (1984a). Neem oil as a vaginal contraceptive. Indian Journal of Medical Research. 79: 131-6.

Sinha, K.C., Riar, S.S., Bardhan, J., Thomas, P., Kain, A.K., & Jain, R.K. (1984b). Anti-implantation effect of neem oil. Indian Journal of Medical Research. (80) 708-10.

Sinha, K.C., & Riar, S.S. (1985). Neem oil-an ideal contraceptive. Biol. Mem. 10(1&2): 107-14.

Sinniah D., & Baskaran, G. (1981). Margosa oil poisoning as a cause of Reye's syndrome. Lancet 1: 487-89.

Sinniah, D., Varghese, G., Baskaran, G., & Koo, S.H. (1983). Fungal flora of neem (Azadirachta indica) seeds and neem oil toxicity. Malay. appl. Biol. 12(1) 1-4: 1-4.

Sinniah, D., Sinniah, D., Sceartz, P.H., Mitchell, R.A., & Areinue, E.L. (1985). Investigation of an animal model of a Reye-like syndrome caused by margosa oil. Pediatric Research 19, 1346-55.

Skellon, J.H., Thorburn, S., Spence, J., & Chatterjee, S.N. (1962). The fatty acids of neem oil and their reduction products. Journal of Scientific Food Agriculture. 13: 639-43.

Stricklen, M., & Saxena, R.C. (1991). Potential for cloning genes from neem for insect resistance in crop plants.

Su, T., & Mulla, M.S. (1998). Ovicidal activity of neem products (azadirachtin) against Culux tarsalis and Culex quinquefasciatus (Diptera: Culicidae). J Am Mosq Control Assoc. Jun; 14(2): 204-9.

Swainalakshmi, T., Gomathi, K., Sulochana, N., Amala Baskar, E., & Parnar, N.S. (1981). Anti-inflammatory activity of (-)-epicatechin, a bioflavonoid isolated from Anacardium occidentale Linn. Indian Journal of Pharmaceutical Sciences.

Talwar, G.P., Pal, R., Singh, O., Garg, S., Tuluva, V., Upadhyay, S.N., Gopalan, S., Jain, V., Kaur, J., & Sehgal, S. (1995). Safety of intrauterine administration of purified neem seed oil (Praneem Vilci) in women and effect of its co-administration with the heterospecies dimer birth control vaccine on antibody response to human chorionic gonadotropin. Indian J Med Res. Aug; 102: 66-70.

Talwar. G.P., Shah, S., Mukherjee, S., & Chabra, R. (1997a). Induced termination of pregnancy by purified extracts of Azadirachta indica (Neem): mechanisms involved. Am J Reprod Immunol. Jun; 37(6): 485-91.

Talwar, G.P., Raghuvanshi, P., Misra, R., Mukherjee, S., & Shah, S. (1997b). Plant immunomodulators for termination of unwanted pregnancy and for contraception and reproductive health. Immunol Cell Biol. Apr; 75(2): 190-2.

Talwar, G.P., Garg, S., Singh, R., Sharma, P.L., Dhar, V., Taluja, V., Dhawan, S. and Upadhyay, S.N. (undated). Praneem polyherbal cream and suppositories. National Institute of Immunology.

Tandan, S.K., Gupta, S., Chandra, S., & Lal, J. (1988). Increasing action of vascular permeability by azadirachta indica seed-oil (neem oil). Indian Journal of Pharm 20: 203-05.

Tandan, S.K., Chandra, S., Gupta, S., Tripathi, H.C., & Lal, J. (1990). Pharmacological effects of azadirachta indica leaves. Fitoterapia. Vol. LXI, (1): 75-8.

Tewari, J.P. (1976). Inhibition of three strains of watermelon mosaic virus by bark extracts. Current Science. 696-7.

Tewari, R.K., Mathur, R., & Prakash, A.O. (1986). Post-coital antifertility effect of neem oil in female albino rats. International Research Communication System of Med Sciences 14:1005-6.

Tewari, R.K., Pathak, S., & Prakash, A.O, (1989). Biochemical and histological studies of reproductive organs in cyclic and ovariectomized rats supporting a non-hormonal action for neem oil. Journal of Ethnopharmacology, 25; 281-93.

Thaker, A.M., & Anjaria, J.V. (1986). Antimicrobial and infected wound healing response of some traditional drugs. Indian Journal of Pharmacology. 171-74.

Thind, T.S., &Dahiya, M.S. (1977). Inhibitory effects of essential oils of four medicinal plants against keratinioholic fungi. East. Pharm. 20: 147-8.

Thompson, E.B., & Anderson, C.C. (1978). Cardiovascular effects of Azadirachta indica extract. J. of Pharmacological Science. 67: 1476-8.

Tirimanna, A.S.L. (1984). Surveying the chemical constituents of neem leaf by two-dimensional thin layer chromatography. In Proceedings of the 2nd International Neem Conference,

Rauischholzhausen, W. Germany. May 25, 1983: 67-74.

Udeinya, I.J. (1993). Anti-malarial activity of Nigerian neem leaves. Transactions of the Royal Society of Tropical Medicine and Hygiene. Vol. 87: 471.

Udeinya, I.J., (1994). Therapeutic compounds derived from the neem tree. U.S. Patent 5,370,873.

Udeinya, I.J., Quakyi, I., Ajayi, F.O., & Brown, N. (unpublished). P. falciparum Gametocyte Inhibition by Neem.

Unander, D.W. Division of Population Oncology, Fox Chase Cancer Center, 7701 Burholme Ave., Philadelphia, PA. 19111. As cited in "Neem - A Tree for Solving Global Problems, National Academy Press, 1992: 62.

Upadhyay, R.K., & Arora, D.K. (1975). Sporostatic nature of neem smoke and its possible ecological influence on air fungal flora of a polluted site. Journal of Scientific Research. Vol. XXVI: 125-9.

Upadhyay, S., Kaushic, C., & Talwar, G.P (1990). Antifertility effects of neem (Azadirachta indica) oil by intrauterine administration: a novel method for contraception. Proceedings of the Royal Society of London. 242: 175-9.

Upadhyay, S., Dhawan, S., Garg, S., & Talwar, G.P. (1992) Immunomodulatory effects of neem (Azadirachta indica) oil. Int J Immunopharmacol. Oct; 14(7):1187-93.

Upadhyay, S.N., Dhawan, S., Garg, S., Wali, N., Tucker, L., & Anderson, D.J. (1993a). Immuno-modulatory properties of neem (azadirachta indica). Proceedings of the World Neem Conference, Bangalore, India. Feb. 24-28, 1993.

Upadhyay, S.N., Dhawan, & Talwar, G.P., (1993b). Antifertility effects of neem (Azadirachta indica) oil in male rats by single intra-vas administration: an alternative approach to vasectomy. J Androl, Jul-Aug; 14(4): 275-81.

Upadhyay, S.N., Dhawan, Sharma, M.G., & Talwar, G.P. (1994). Long term contraceptive effects of intrauterine neem treatment (IUNT) in bonnet monkeys: an alternative to intrauterine contraceptive devices (IUCD). Contraception Feb; 49: 161-9.

Uwaifo, A.O. (1984). The mutagenicities of seven coumarin derivatives and furan derivatives (nimbolide) isolated from three medicinal plants. Journal of Toxicology and Environmental Health. 13: 521-30.

Van der Nat, J.M., Van der Sluis, W.G. de Haan, A.H.J.M., de Silva, K.T.D., & Labadie, R.P. (1986). Ethnopharmacological study of azadirachta indica. A conceptual evaluation. Plant Medicines. (6): 552.

Van der Nat, J.M., Klerx, J.P.A.M., Van Dijk, H., De Silva, K.T.D., & Labadie, R.P. (1987). Immunomodulatory activity of aqueous extract of Azadirachta indica stem bark. Journal of Ethnopharmacology 19: 125-31.

Van der Nat, J.M., 't Hart, L.A., Vander Sluis, W.G., Van Dijk, H., Van den Berg, A.J.J., De Silva, K.T.D., & Labadie, R.P. (1989a). Characterization of anti-complement compounds from Azadirachta indica, Journal of Ethnopharmacology 27: 15-24.

Van der Nat, J.M., van der Sluis, W.G., 't Hart, L.A., van Dijk, H., de Silva, K.T.D., & Labadie, R.P. (1989b) Four chemiluminescence-inhibitory phenolic compounds from Azadirachta indica bark. Planta Medica, (55): 108.

Van der Nat, J.M., van der Sluis, W.G., t' Hart, L.A., van Dijk, H., de Silva, K.T.D., & Labadie, R.P. (1991). Activity-guided isolation and identification of Azadirachta indica A. Juss. (Meliaceae) bark extract constituents, which specifically inhibit human polymorphonuclear leukocytes. Planta Medica, in press.

Varghese, G., Baskaran, G., & Koos., S.H. (1983). Fungal flora of neem (Azadirachta indica) seeds and neem oil toxicity. Malays. Appl. Biol. 12: 1-4.

Vashi, I.G., & Patel, H.C. (1988). Amino acids content and microbial activity of azadirachta indica A juss. Journal of Inst. Chemists (India) Vol. 60. 43-4.

Vijayalakshmi, K., Gaur, H.S., & Gosuremi, B.K. (1985). Neem for the control of plant parasitic nematodes. Neem Newsletter 2: 35-42.

Vohora, S.B. (1986). What is purification of blood? Hamdard. Vol XXVIII, (1): 72-84.

Wachsman M.B., Damonte, E.B., Coto, C.E., & de Torres, R.A. (1987). Antiviral effects of Melia azedarach L. leaves extracts on Sindbis virus-infected cells. Antiviral Res. Aug; 8(1):1-12.

Wachsman M.B., & Coto, C.E. (1995). Susceptibility of picornaviruses++ to an antiviral of plant origin (meliacin). Rev Argent Microbiol. Jan-Mar; 27(1): 33-7.

Wachsman, M.B., Castilla, V., & Coto, C.E. (1998). Inhibition of foot and mouth disease virus (FMDV) uncoating by a plant-derived peptide isolated from Melia azedarach L leaves. Arch Virol. 143(3): 581-90.

Wagh, Shrikant, Y. (1988). Clinical studies in viral hepatitis. Deerghayu International; 4 (4): 17-19.

Wali, N., Dhawan, S., Garg, S., Upadhyay, S.N. (1993). Anti inflammatory effect of neem leaf extract. Proceedings of the World Neem Conference, Bangalore, India. Feb. 24-28, 1993.

Walton, S.F., Myerscough, M.R., & Currie, B.J. (2000). Studies I vitro on the relative efficacy of current acaricides for Sarcoptes scabiei var. hominis. Trans R Soc Trop Med Hyg. Jan-Feb; 94(1): 92-6.

Wolinsky, L.E., Mania, S., Nachani, S., & Ling, S. (1996). The inhibiting effect of aqueous Azadirachta indica (neem) extract upon bacterial properties influencing in vitro plaque formation. J Dent Res. Feb; 75(2): 816-22.

Yadav, S.K., & Rathore, J.S. (1976). Mitotic inhibition by Melia azadirachta leaf extracts. Proc. Nat. Acad. Sci., India, Vol. 46(b). IV: 527-8.

Zeppenfeldt, H. (news release - Dr. Grandel) Deflator et protector Paractol - flussig der Deutsche apotheker. "Neem extrakt - ein interessanter wirkstoff fur die zahn - und mundhygiene.

Herbs and other natural health products and information are often available at natural food stores or metaphysical bookstores. If you cannot find what you need locally, you can contact one of the following sources of supply.

Sources of Supply:

The following companies have an extensive selection of useful products and a long track-record of fulfillment. They have natural body care, aromatherapy, flower essences, crystals and tumbled stones, homeopathy, herbal products, vitamins and supplements, videos, books, audio tapes, candles, incense and bulk herbs, teas, massage tools and products and numerous alternative health items across a wide range of categories.

WHOLESALE:

Wholesale suppliers sell to stores and practitioners, not to individual consumers buying for their own personal use. Individual consumers should contact the RETAIL supplier listed below. Wholesale accounts should contact with business name, resale number or practitioner license in order to obtain a wholesale catalog and set up an account.

Lotus Light Enterprises, Inc.
P O Box 1008 NUH
Silver Lake, WI 53170 USA
262 889 8501 (phone)
262 889 8591 (fax)
800 548 3824 (toll free order line)

RETAIL:

Retail suppliers provide products by mail order direct to consumers for their personal use. Stores or practitioners should contact the wholesale supplier listed above.

Internatural
33719 116th Street NUH
Twin Lakes, WI 53181 USA
800 643 4221 (toll free order line)
262 889 8581 office phone
EMAIL: internatural@lotuspress.com
WEB SITE: www.internatural.com

Web site includes an extensive annotated catalog of more than 10,000 items that can be ordered "on line" for your convenience 24 hours a day, 7 days a week.

THE YOGA OF HERBS
An Ayurvedic Guide to
Herbal Medicine

For the first time, a book is available which offers a detailed understanding and classification of herbs, utilizing the ancient system of Ayurveda. This fully developed and theoretically articulated medical system developed in India has proved itself effective for more than 5000 years as that country's classical healing tradition.

There are more than 230 herbs listed, with 88 herbs explained in detail. Included are nearly all the most commonly used western herbs according to a new and profound Ayurvedic perspective. Also a number of special powerful Ayurvedic herbs are introduced for the first time. The book is over 250 pages, with beautiful diagrams and lengthy charts, as well as a detailed glossary and index to further enhance and clarify the text.

The book combines the knowledge and experience of two respected authors in the realm of the spiritual and medical sciences of India.

Dr. Michael Tierra, Herbalist, and author of *The Way of Herbs*, says in the Foreword to this book:

> "Dr. Lad and Mr. Frawley have made a truly powerful contribution to alternative, natural health care by their creation of this important book.
>
> This book for the first time will serve not only to make Ayurvedic medicine of greater practical value to Westerners but, in fact, ultimately advance the whole system of Western herbalism forward into greater effectiveness. I think anyone interested in herbs should closely study this book whether their interests lie in Western herbology, traditional Chinese herbology or in Ayurvedic medicine."

Contents include • The Ayurvedic Theory of Herbal Medicine • How to Prepare and Use Herbs According to Ayurveda • Spiritual Usages of Herbs • How to Use Herbs According to Individual Constitutional Needs • How to Approach Western Herbs According to Ayurvedic Medical Principles • and much more.

PUBLISHED BY LOTUS PRESS
To order your copy, send $14.95 (postpaid) to:
Lotus Press
P.O. Box 325-CTM
Twin Lakes, WI 53181
Request our complete book & sidelines catalog
Wholesale inquiries welcome.

Back to Eden
Revised & Updated Edition

by Jethro Kloss

If you are interested in simple and effective alternatives to today's expensive and impersonal high technology, try this classic and comprehensive guide for safe and inexpensive natural remedies for the prevention of disease and sickness.

In Jethro Kloss's words, "God has provided a remedy for every disease that may afflict us. If our scientists would put forth the same efforts to find the 'true remedies' of nature that they do in the manipulation of chemicals, we would soon find the use of poisonous drugs and chemicals eliminated and sickness would be rare indeed."

Over **5 million** copies sold and still selling strong. This book is one of those rare phenomena which are truly epoch making – beginning an era of health based on natural living.

Trade Paper	ISBN	0-940985-09-8	936p	$14.95
Hardcover	ISBN	0-940985-13-6	936p	$21.95
Mass Market	ISBN	0-940985-10-1	936p	$ 9.95

Available at bookstores and natural food stores nationwide, or order your copy directly by sending the appropriate amount for the binding of your choice plus $2.50 shipping/handling ($.75 s/h for each additional copy ordered at the same time) to:

Lotus Press, P O Box 325, Twin Lakes, WI 53181 USA
toll free order line: 800 824 6396   office phone: 262 889 8561
office fax: 262 889 8591   email: lotuspress@lotuspress.com
web site: www.lotuspress.com

Lotus Press is the publisher of a wide range of books and software in the field of alternative health, including Ayurveda, Chinese medicine, herbology, aromatherapy, Reiki and energetic healing modalities. Request our free book catalog.

Ayurveda, Nature's Medicine

by Dr. David Frawley & Dr. Subhash Ranade

Ayurveda, Natures Medicine is an excellent introduction to the full field of Ayurvedic Medicine from diet and herbs to yoga and massage. It has a notable emphasis on practical self-care and daily life regimens that makes it helpful for everyone seeking health and wholeness. The book is an excellent primer for students beginning in the field and wanting to have a firm foundation to understand the entire system.

Trade Paper   ISBN 0-914955-95-0   368 pp pb $19.95

Available at bookstores and natural food stores nationwide or order your copy directly by sending $19.95 plus $2.50 shipping/handling ($.75 s/h for each additional copy ordered at the same time) to:

Lotus Press, P O Box 325, Twin Lakes, WI 53181 USA
toll free order line: 800 824 6396 office phone: 262 889 8561
office fax: 262 889 8591 email: lotuspress@lotuspress.com
web site: www.lotuspress.com

Lotus Press is the publisher of a wide range of books and software in the field of alternative health, including Ayurveda, Chinese medicine, herbology, aromatherapy, Reiki and energetic healing modalities. Request our free book catalog.